IF I'M HONEST...

A No BS Guide to Loving Yourself,
Navigating Relationships
and Trusting the Journey

Dina Strada

IF I'M HONEST/Dina Strada 1ˢᵗ Edition
ISBN 979-8-9891382-0-3

If I'm Honest

For Logan and Kaia,

May you always be able to be honest with me, yourselves, and everyone in your life about how you feel and who you truly are. I love you more than you'll ever know.

and

For Mom and Dad,

Thank you for always believing in me
and supporting my dreams.
I finally did it!

Dina Strada

Foreword

If I'm honest, the first time I read Dina's words I was immediately smitten by her ability to reach the reader with a compelling blend of humor and frankness. I'd never encountered such vulnerability, or a natural way of sharing deeply personal experiences, without it being burdensome. In fact, everything Dina wrote was relatable and imminently helpful. Needless to say, many others felt the same way, as witnessed by the hundreds of comments left by Dina's appreciative audience. (or, left in Dina's many published articles)

Anais Nin once wrote, "the role of the writer is not to say what we can all say, but what we are unable to say." This, for me, is the epitome of Dina's writing. She does not shy away from the truth of life, the conundrum of being human; but courageously steps into the messiness and beauty of it all. She stirs the cauldron of emotions with grace, then spills some ink so we can make sense of it all within our own lives.

What stands out most for me is that I can trust Dina's words, because they come from her own experience, unfiltered, often raw, always deeply self-reflective. There's an art to that, but I doubt that Dina would admit to it, because as much as she is sassy and bold, she is also very much humbly concerned with being of service. And that's exactly what this book accomplishes.

If I'm Honest tells it like it is. It allows us to see ourselves with clarity. It also helps us find the humor in our foibles, no judgment, just acceptance of the fact that life is messy, and weird, and worth every effort we put into it. Dina helps us find comfort in the uncomfortable, laughter in the tragedy, gratitude in the moments that fortify our soul.

The truth is, we're all moving through the same things in life, to varying degrees. It's easy to feel alone in the process, or to be harsh with ourselves. Dina creates community with her essays. The many laugh-out-loud moments, groaning-to-self moments, and oh-my-god-that's-so-me moments bring everything into perspective. Dina can laugh at herself, and that gives us permission to do the same. She holds up a compassionate mirror – the gift of a truly empathic writer.

I hope you find yourself in these pages and love yourself fiercely. I hope you will see your life with kindness. I hope that you will see others in their vulnerability and know them to be just like you.

If I'm Honest leads us toward wholeness. Not perfection, wholeness - because it accepts the human condition as a journey along many paths, all leading home.

~ Monika Carless, *teacher of the Wise Woman Path. Hay House author of Transforming the Mother Wound - Practices for Healing Your Inner Wise Woman Using Rituals and Grounded Spirituality; release, spring 2024, and, The Dark Pool Trilogy, an unashamed fairy tale for grown-ass adults.*

p.s. Dina, I'm never forgiving you for meeting Brad Pitt. I've been letting my freak flag fly for years and no Brad. (Reader, see Chapter 25)

Contents

Introduction

"So, when are you gonna write a book?" my 5th grade teacher, Miss Dempsey asked.

This was years ago. At that point one of my elementary school friends who was also in her 5th grade class had published her first children's book and she dropped that little tidbit of info to fuel the flames under my procrastinating ass.

"Oh, I'll get to it. Work is just crazy," I'd lie. Work being "crazy" is my all-time favorite excuse for everything.

I mean, I was crazy at work. I'm *always* crazy at work. If I waited to not be crazed at work to write a book, this book would be coming out when I was 85.

"How's your book going?" my best friend, Elizabeth would ask. I would think about lying and telling her I had been diligently working on it at night when the kids were in bed, but then she'd do something sneaky like ask me to send some of it to her so she could read it, which I couldn't possibly do since I had done absolutely *nada* on the writing front. So, I'd roll out my list of excuses instead.

"Well, um, I really haven't done much because work is crazy (favorite excuse) and I'm not feeling inspired and besides I'm writing articles all the time, so I feel like, what more is there to say that I haven't already said? And besides, *who am I to write a book?* I mean, I'm a nobody. It would be a complete waste of my time anyway. I'm probably just going to stick to writing articles."

Intense stare from Lizzie. "Okaaayyyy," she'd singsong in her sweet, non-judgmental voice. "I just think you have a lot of wisdom people could benefit from and it would be a shame for you to not share that with people."

"I will," I'd lie. "When work isn't so crazy."

Over the years, multitudes of other friends, coaching clients, family members and co-workers I had been telling that I was going to write a book someday would lob the same question at me. "When is the book coming out?"

More excuses I actually started to believe, "I'm working on it," (lie) "It's not the right time" (never is) "I don't want to write one," (fear). Until one day I finally realized...

Girrrrrrrrl, you are so full of it. Just do the damn thing already!

So, here it is. I did the damn thing. I should start off by saying that *if I'm honest....* I'm not going to talk about certain parts of my life that lots of people thought I should talk about.

There, I said it. Why lie?

Whoever coined the term "zero f*cks" is definitely a Millennial. I give many f*cks. I care what people think. I was afraid people would screen shot passages of some of my more vulnerable confessions and text each other... "OMG what a LOSER!"

I was concerned I'd write about certain parts of my life that I'm not proud of and people would judge me. I didn't want to come across as too "woo woo" or preachy because I hate people who try to convince me that having what I want is as easy as just "closing your eyes, visualizing it and it will magically manifest!" I'm a little "woo woo" but I'm still a practical Jersey girl at heart who believes getting what we want involves a lot of hard work.

Then there are my kids. I've run around the house for the last year declaring my book is going to be on the *New York Times* bestseller list, so they better be nice to me before I become big and famous and am interviewed by Hoda and Jenna on the TODAY show and now that I've gotten them all hyped about the book, I have to assume they're going to actually want to read the book. With that being said, I chose not to share certain parts of my life out of respect for them. So kids, mommy left out a bunch of juicy stories I really wanted to tell but I didn't want to emotionally traumatize you. You can thank me later.

Anyway, the book is titled, *If I'm Honest* because I'm honest about a whole bunch of other stuff I *was* willing to talk about even though at times it was hard. Like how I still feel like I'm a loser because I'm divorced, and how people who tell me aging is a beautiful thing and I need to accept my crow's feet and crepey skin need to shut up already, and that parenting is really hard and anyone telling you they love it and it's *the most rewarding thing* ever are full of shit.

They aren't telling you the whole story. I'm gonna tell you the whole story.

I feel it's important to talk about the hard stuff, the stuff we all struggle with.
The things we believe only we are going through,
the secrets we carry,
the imperfect way we do life,
how hard it is to trust ourselves and accept some people and situations as being exactly what they are.

You aren't alone. I see you.

If you're worried you're doing life wrong, screwing up all your relationships, carrying around a boatload of shame and can't figure out how to give yourself a break, I've got you. I've been there and I don't have it all figured out either. But I've gathered a whole lot of wisdom along the way doing what doesn't work and figuring out what does. I'm living proof you can make questionable choices, be a hot mess for a while, hit rock bottom and still pick yourself up and be just fine.

In fact, you can be pretty damn fabulous even when your life looks like a complete mess. Truthfully, barely anyone is paying attention to you anyway.

If I'm Honest is not an instruction manual or a "how I screwed up and triumphed" hero's journey. It's more of a "hey let's get real about life" convo. It's a *how not to do* relationships guide because remember, I'm single and definitely know *how not to do things*! It's an invitation to be your bad self, even when you're unsure who that is. It's a permission slip to not to be perfect, do you and be proud of that.

And if I'm really honest...I'm so glad this book is finally written. Now I can go back to procrastinating doing other things that are hard since if you must know, work is absolutely crazy.

Section 1

Loving Ourselves

Chapter 1
Self-Care is Not What You Think

If I'm honest, I think self-care is the one thing most women, and even men fail miserably at. We can rule the world, yet we can't find the time to give ourselves small breaks to make sure we're nurturing ourselves while doing it.

I start every day with the intention of doing at least one thing to take care of myself and I admit, I often fail miserably.

There are too many things to get done, a never ending to do list that grows by the hour, emails that need to be answered, kids that need to be fed and dropped off somewhere, work deadlines I need to hit and not enough hours in the day.

My intentions are good, my execution just needs some work.

I have a friend who keep a ginormous white-board with a long list of what needs to get done on a Saturday hanging in her kitchen and my first thought when I look at that thing is, *"For the love of God, why does any of that shit need to get done and that is definitely not the first thing I want to stare at when I wake up in the morning!"* That same friend pops Adderall and drinks a bottle of wine every night which is her form of self-care, but I argue it's the never-ending to do list pushing her over the edge.

I don't have a white board, but I'm guilty of thinking my long list of to-dos are so important, I'm willing to sacrifice meals, sleep, slowing down to rest for 5 minutes or doing anything fun with my weekend just to check them off and be able to say they were done. Now the only list I keep is scribbled on a post it note and typically includes no more than 3 things I'll do whenever I get to it.

So many of us struggle with self-care. We think the whole idea is plain old indulgent. For years I thought self-care meant a day at the spa, getting my nails done or running away for a weekend with my girlfriends (all fabulous ways to self-care by the way).

But that's not the self-care I'm talking about. As I've gotten older, I've realized that women especially are so exhausted and stressed out because we're trying to be *everything, all the time to everyone* and that shit has gotta stop.

The self-care I'm talking about is unsexy as hell and absolutely essential. It's filling our own cup before we even *think* about doing a damn thing for anyone else.

It's taking a few quiet minutes in the morning to drink our cup of coffee or tea and eat something before we jump into work emails, make breakfast for our spouse or kids or dog, start reading texts and emails, making phone calls, and tackling the day.

It's taking a walk or putting in a sweaty workout no matter what's on our to-do list because our bodies are temples that need to be cherished and taken care of so we can take care of everything and everyone else that needs our attention.

It's taking mandated breaks from the phone, saying "no I can't today", and then plopping down on the couch in your coziest sweats and reading *Us Weekly* or binge watching *Vanderpump Rules*.

It's setting boundaries with your time. It's saying no to everyone and everything even if it's not what they want to hear. It's shutting the laptop off and saying no to work when it doesn't need to be done right now. It's taking the vacation. It's not allowing what other people say and do affect you.

It's not comparing yourself with someone else. It's taking breaks from social media and realizing what's in your feed is very often fake news.

It's not falling into the trap of believing that everything is all on you. Or that you need to live up to some internal pressure you're putting on yourself to keep up with the Joneses. It's letting the laundry pile up and your house stay dirty and getting OK with not needing the external to look perfect.

I've spent a lifetime not doing these things. There are days I run myself so far up my own ass I want to collapse.   I believe the sink can't have a dirty dish in it, the pantry needs to be fully stocked, my parents need me to stop by and do something for them, a friend needs me to respond to their text right that second, work emails need to be responded to at 10:00 at night and saying no would mean letting everyone down.

But I'm a work in progress. I've gotten much better over the years and have worked daily self-care rituals into my routine that happen no matter what I have on my plate.

Things I try to do every day that anyone can adopt into their own schedule:

- *Praying for 5 minutes before I get out of bed.*
- *Journaling for 10 minutes while I drink my morning cup of coffee.*
- *Working up a sweat every single day.*
- *Walking at least 10,000 steps.*
- *Reading 10 pages of something that brings me joy before I go to bed.*
- *Eating at least 2 healthy meals a day sitting down instead of shoving food down my mouth on the run. And if I'm on the run, that food is always still healthy.*
- *Getting at least 7-8 hours of sleep.*

Your self-care rituals will be different than mine or anyone else's. But it's important to figure out what *you* need to fill your own cup every day whether that's more sleep, taking a walk, fueling your body more often, connecting with a friend, getting outside, delegating work, meditating, or locking yourself in your closet and hiding from the world (that can be the best self-care of all)! Write those things down and make it a priority every single day to do them.

The best way I've learned we can truly take care of ourselves though is to ASK FOR HELP when we need it.

Real self-care, the very best kind, is asking for what we need when we need it. Yes, you can do it too. I used to think it made me look weak or was an admittance that I wasn't superwoman when I asked for help but I'm *not* superwoman, and I've got nothing to prove anymore.

And you know what? People genuinely feel good when they can do something to help you. I love it when someone feels comfortable enough with me to ask for my help. Giving for me feels so much more rewarding than receiving and makes me feel more comfortable receiving help from another person when I need it. It's a beautiful exchange of energy.

As you read this book, my intention is that you'll take away little nuggets of ways you can work self-care for your soul into your own life; from learning how to set better boundaries with people, to protecting your heart in relationships, to letting go of perfectionism, and learning how to embrace and accept every experience in your life as being exactly the way it's meant to be happening in this moment.

These are the first steps to self-care.

Chapter 2
Perfection is Overrated

If I'm honest, there are days I still strive to be perfect, knowing full well there's no such thing. Now I just aim for progress, knowing that's as close to perfection as anyone can get.

The first time I heard the phrase, "Progress, not perfection" I was sitting on an uncomfortable folding chair in a church basement on 76th and Broadway in NYC.

I had hit rock bottom in my endless quest for the perfect body. The battle had started my sophomore year in high school, haunted me all through college and had now followed me into young adulthood. Endless hours of secretly hiding my daily battle of starving myself, counting calories, back-to-back workout classes and then binging and purging when I made one slip up on my diet had me in a deep depression. I needed help. At the time 12 Step programs were all the rage and besides, it was the only type of help I could afford on my $23,000 a year salary.

I was sick of myself. At the age of 24, I was sick of the way I was treating myself and my body. I honestly couldn't remember a time when I wasn't trying so hard. Trying to be thin, trying to be good, trying to get perfect grades, trying to be agreeable, trying to be liked, trying to be enough, trying to fit in, trying to be prettier, trying to be the perfect friend.

It was an exhausting amount of trying.

Flash forward 10 years later and I was still engaging in the same unhealthy behaviors. I was working obscene production hours at the movie studio where I worked, constantly under pressure and stressed out trying to please everyone around me, my boss, my colleagues, the artists I worked with. I held myself up to a standard of perfection no human being could possibly meet. By then I was married and on top of trying to be the perfect wife I was still trying to be that perfect employee, the perfect daughter, the perfect friend or whatever I believed people wanted me to be.

You can only engage in this bullshit, disempowering behavior for so long before your body tells you it's had enough. The body keeps the score. My relentless behavior of never giving myself a break led to another relapse into my eating disorder after many years of abstinence and recovery, another stint in the 12-step program, a short-term medical leave from my job after a debilitating bout with chronic fatigue, depression, and a "what-the-hell-am I doing with my life" midlife crisis at the tender age of 34.

It was only after my marriage fell apart and I got divorced, an unimaginable humiliating horror I never imagined that perfect little me, who played by all the rules would go through, that I started to do the deep inner work of healing my, "I'm not enough" story. Believing I wasn't "enough" had led me to making so many bad decisions, based in fear.

If I don't marry this person I'm with right now, I may never have kids.

If I don't work 14 hours a day, they'll think I'm not committed to the job.

If I say no, I'll let them down.

If I speak up, they'll get upset with me.

It was not just exhausting but inauthentic. I realized I was living at least half my life not being myself. The real me was messy and imperfect. The real me got pissed off at times and wanted to speak up for myself but was too afraid of confrontation.

The real me didn't want to do a lot of things I was told I had to do like dress a certain way at work or conform to fit in. The real me didn't want to stay out late or go to parties I had no interest in going to. The real me hated excel spreadsheets, pretending I wanted to "be a leader" and having to act a certain way at work if I wanted to rise up the corporate ladder. The real me was tired of having to twist myself into someone I wasn't to feel like I was "enough".

So, I started doing the deep inner work to heal all that bullshit. When I say, I did the *deep inner work*, people ask me what that means. Listen, I lived in LA, land of the woo woo. My NJ friends and family like to make fun of California people but those people know where it's at when it comes to healing and being a little more open minded. I had access to it all, so I pretty much did it. Don't judge me. I mean of course some of you will but whatever, it worked for me.

I found a great therapist, went to OA (Overeaters Anonymous) meetings, did the Landmark Forum, attended a Wanderlust conference in Palm Springs, binge watched videos of Gabby Bernstein, Dr. Wayne Dyer, Deepak Chopra, Joe Dispenza, and any other spiritual teacher I could find on You tube, read shitloads of self-help books, joined a women's circle, attended yoga, writing, and personal development retreats, sat with grandmother (plant medicine) and even stared into stranger's eyes to "connect" and "get in touch with my feelings" which was totally uncomfortable and made me feel like a total dork. But I did it anyway.

And after all of that, I finally learned to accept my body no matter what I weigh and love myself unconditionally.

HA...NOT! I mean, come on, I said I wasn't perfect.

Listen, I still don't love my body. People are surprised to hear this but I'm giving you one of my best kept secrets here. I long to look like a 5'11" Victoria Secret model but instead I still clock in at only 4'11" and have legs like a gymnast. And body aside, I still have character flaws that drive myself and other people crazy that I continue to work on. But I accept myself for who I am and because of that, I don't expect anyone else in my life to be perfect either.

The more we demand perfection from ourselves, the more we expect perfection from other people. If we're holding ourselves up to an impossible standard, the tendency will be to hold the people in our lives up to that same impossible standard. Let's face it, if we can't be messy and complicated and screw up sometimes, then we're not giving any free passes out to anyone else either!

And that's when our relationships fall apart... when we have the expectation that people in our lives need to be a certain way to make us happy and never screw up. Nobody in this world is perfect or immune from making mistakes.

People make mistakes. Loads of them. Our romantic partners and spouses will do and say things that hurt us. Our friends will let us down at times. Our parents may have made choices when we were growing up that hurt us or affected us negatively in some way.

It's part of being human. I like to think I'm a pretty exceptional and kind human being and I've done lots of things that have hurt people unintentionally. Whether that's something I've said or done or not done, I look back on my life and wish there were things I could take back or go back and do differently.

What I know for sure is I'm doing the best I can in every moment. Every night when I rest my head on the pillow I think about my day and know I did the very best I could. Isn't that what every single one of us is doing?

So, for the love of God, please give yourself a break. It's OK to make mistakes.

Forgive yourself. Move on. Let things go.

Forgive others. Move on. Let things go.

One of my favorite Maya Angelou quotes is, "When we know better, we do better." And I believe we do. With experience comes wisdom and the more we try and fail, the more we make mistakes, the more wisdom we carry in our back pockets to do things better next time around.

One of the secrets I've learned to being truly happy is letting go of any expectations I have about myself. As long as we're on this earth, we're learning, growing works in progress. Our souls are here for that reason alone - growth. So, remain open to the lessons, knowing each one brings you just a little bit closer to fully stepping into who you're meant to be.

If you can focus on that, and the fact that making mistakes is all part of your growth, then being perfect serves no real purpose anyway. If you're making progress every day, you're on the right track along with the rest of us imperfect human beings.

Dina Strada

Chapter 3
Here's What Happens When You Stop Hating Yourself

If I'm honest, I love myself more today because I've learned to accept every part of myself, even the less than perfect parts.

Ok maybe I don't love them as much as I loved my hot, toned muscular wrinkle-free appearance of my youth, but I don't obsess anymore over every single imperfection. (just a couple).

That doesn't mean I don't have moments where I look in the mirror and think, "OMG, what the hell is happening here!!" More on that later. At my age, it's inevitable when another deep line crops up out of nowhere around the eyes, more loose skin appears to be hanging from my neck or I'm having a really bad hair day.

But it's not about my looks anyway. I'm proud of the woman I've become over the years. Even though I can still be impatient, overly sensitive and a little too direct at times, I accept those things as not who I am, but how I'm behaving in the moment and then try to understand why I'm behaving that way so I can shift it. Rather than hate myself, I've learned how to find compassion for myself so I'm not constantly berating myself for a bad day, a bad decision or a less than stellar moment.

This shift didn't happen overnight. For over 2 decades, I've worked in the personal development space. I've actively sought out teachers, mentors, therapists, and friends who call me out on my shit and don't allow me to engage in any behaviors that aren't kind and loving to myself.

It's work. If we want to get there, we need to be willing to do the actual work.

But the work, no matter how long it takes (and my belief is there's no finish line, it's a daily practice), is worth it. Do you really want to spend your days picking yourself apart and not accepting who you are when you could be in full expression of who you truly are every day?

Because here's the thing that happens when you stop hating yourself...

You make better choices. You put up with less. You choose yourself more. You release old self-destructive patterns and replace them with loving ones. You stop making excuses for other people who are shitty and the things in your life that aren't OK.

When I really learned to love myself, things changed. *I changed.* I'm sometimes floored with how differently I move through the world now.

I don't engage with anybody wasting my time or not treating me with respect. This goes in the workplace and in personal relationships. If someone doesn't treat me with kindness or is playing games with me, I'm out.

When you no longer hate yourself, you don't need to lash out. The days of screaming at another person about how much they suck and why they don't treat you better become a thing of the past.

Nope, you just don't engage anymore. You quietly walk away with no anger or resentment in your heart. You don't reach out because you miss them. You don't get hooked again when they text you or ask you for something you simply don't want to give.

When you no longer hate yourself, you stop judging other people. You don't really care anymore what other people are doing because *you're doing you*, they're doing them, and there's a certain amount of empathy and compassion you now have for others because you finally have it for yourself.

When you no longer hate yourself, you don't drink in excess, do illegal street drugs, overeat or undereat.

You no longer think a bottle of wine, a bag of chips, a hit of cocaine or sleeping with a total stranger is going to make you feel better. You stop making excuses for not moving your body and make time to take care of yourself physically, mentally, and spiritually even the days it's really f*cking hard.

When you no longer hate yourself, you become accountable.

If you want to reach a goal or accomplish something, you put a plan in place to be accountable to someone. If you're drinking too much, you join AA. If you're unhappy with some aspect of your life, you seek out a therapist or whatever works for you and do the actual work. You stop doing life alone. When we stop hating ourselves, we let other people in to help. No more secrets. No more hiding.

When you no longer hate yourself, you set boundaries.

You set boundaries with your time, with your family, in your relationships. You set boundaries at work so you can show up every day as your best self. You stop saying yes to things because you want to people please. You stop believing that if you say no, you're a bad person and people won't like you.

When you no longer hate yourself, you don't beat yourself up when you make mistakes.

You don't have the expectation that you need to be perfect to be loved. You stop working hard to be liked. You settle into yourself, into the feeling that being you is enough.

I was thinking one day about a man I really connected with right after I moved back to NJ. I've met maybe one or two people in the past 2 years that have caught my attention, made my heart skip a beat. He was one of them.

Of course, he wasn't available. Well, he was when he first asked me out, then never followed up and met someone else. I was disappointed, even a little angry as the months went by and his situation didn't change. I kept thinking, "I wouldn't have met him if this wasn't going to be something, so he'll be available soon if I just wait it out!" I knew he had similar feelings for me, but as time went on and he stayed in his current relationship, I realized I had to let it go.

When you no longer hate yourself though, you don't think, "What's wrong with me? Why don't things ever work out for me? Why don't they choose me?" Nope. Wanna know what I think?
If not this, something better.

It's not always about you.

Us not getting everything we want in life doesn't have to be some bullshit story we're carrying around about not being enough or the world being so unfair that we don't get what we want.

Maybe it's not our time. Maybe it's not the right thing for you at this moment. Maybe it's coming later. Maybe you're just too damn fabulous and that thing you so desperately want isn't aligned with your fabulousness!

When we no longer hate ourselves...well, the world opens up in beautiful ways.

Chapter 4
For the Love of God, What's Up with My Face, Body, All of It?

If I'm honest, I'll never be one of those women who ages gracefully and brags about how fabulous I'm getting the older I get. I've got a mirror folks and it tells a different story.

This book is called *If I'm Honest* for a reason. I'm not going to sugar coat it. I'm completely OK telling you that I absolutely hate getting older and I doubly hate what it's doing to my face, body, neck, and everything else gravity is taking along for the ride.

I remember Oprah Winfrey in an interview with Tina Fey who was just turning 50, sharing what Maya Angelou once said to her. She told Oprah, "*Babe, the fifties are everything you've been meaning to be. It's everything you thought you might do. This is it. It's coming in. You're not even there yet.*"

I love this. I love and appreciate Maya's wisdom. This is truly the decade where I see myself becoming everything I've always intended to be in the world and no longer waiting or making excuses to do the things I've dreamed of doing.

She did not, however, mention anything about the body parts that start becoming unrecognizable.

Maya, I love you and I mostly love that you shared only what is truly important to focus on as we grow older. But someone has to get real about the physical changes and challenges we all start to see on the outside as we're finally becoming our best selves on the inside.

Prior to getting a little older, I would never have used the word *vain* to describe myself. I was never the super-hot girl growing up, but I got my share of lingering stares and catcalls when I passed by a group of men. My friends and I would be disgusted by this unwanted display of attention. I'd shoot the men a dirty look and hurry past. "The nerve, staring at me like that!"

Now I'd *kill* to be stared at appreciatively for more than a few lingering seconds. I'd give up my morning cup of coffee for eternity to hear a whistle as I sauntered past a group of men. For the love of God, why are men not falling at my feet anymore?

Well, I'll tell you why. I've become invisible. That's what happens at a certain age.

I know what some of you are thinking. I'm being dramatic and also not spreading a body positive message here. I'm not focusing on how much wisdom, maturity, self-awareness, and life-experience we have at a certain age that makes aging one of the most beautiful experiences ever.

Listen, I know it's an honor and privilege every day to wake up and be healthy and breathing. I'm truly grateful God has blessed me with this beautiful life I get to live. But that's for another chapter. Let's get real ladies... none of us takes our health for granted. But are you really embracing that spare tire around your midsection? How about the sagging neckline? Stretch marks from pregnancy? Varicose veins? Cellulite? What about those gorgeous deep wrinkles around your mouth and eyes? Sexy, huh?

I think not.

I'm about to get real about what's happening to my face, body, and self-esteem as I'm aging because I know I'm not alone and I don't want you to feel alone either. I've watched interviews and read countless articles written by other women brave enough to talk about this very thing and admit they too are struggling and as a society, we need to be able to talk about it.

I'm not afraid to admit I've gotten more insecure and less confident when it comes to my looks. I'm fit and in shape, yet I find myself hiding behind baggy shirts and covering up more because I'm self-conscious about my looser skin. I highlight my hair to hide the random grays. I've gotten Botox to soften the wrinkles around my eyes. I've filled the lines around my lips and mouth to replace the lost collagen that's making my face move further and further south.
On the flip side, I try to focus on what's real in my life. The things that matter. When I wake up every morning, before I even open my eyes, I pray. Usually, it's just for the simple things like a good night's sleep, the feeling of my daughter's body next to mine if she's crawled into my bed in the middle of the night, or my son's hug before he heads to the bus stop.

Then I stumble out of bed, make my way to the bathroom to brush my teeth and even though the same person staring back at me in the mirror is the same one as the night before, I look up and shout, "OMG holy hell, when did *that* happen?" I shove my face closer to the magnifying mirror where I spot a new piece of hair growing out of my chin or wrinkles under my eyes that seem to have etched themselves deeper into my skin overnight.

I won't get into the unruly random gray hairs that have a life of their own, sprouting from the top of my head like a neglected garden that hasn't been weeded since last spring.

I don't know if you feel this way, but the slow change in my appearance seems to have happened overnight. One day I was young and still admiring my flat stomach from daily workouts and my shiny, full head of hair and the next day, I was avoiding the mirror altogether. It wasn't the turning of a certain age that brought on this feeling or change in my appearance. I think it's been a slow evolution that happened over time and one day I woke up and just *noticed it*.

Even younger women are now being targeted by the beauty industry to do something called "preventative aging". A 22-year-old girl I met at a retreat shared that she is already getting ads in her social media feed for Botox and fillers to prevent wrinkles. (*Girls – save yourself the time and money and don't feed into this bullshit!*)

Slap on some good sunblock and call it a day. Wear a hat when you're out in the sun. Eat well. Drink loads of water. Move your body. Don't smoke and say no to drugs. Get enough sleep. Reduce your stress. All those things alone will go a long way in preserving your youthful glow.

I have always been honest with friends about the procedures I've tried to look better and feel better. Because I work so hard to *feel* good by eating healthy, working out, getting enough sleep, and taking care of my emotional health, I want the outside to match the inside. I want to look good for my age and I don't want to feel invisible.

At the same time, I want to find acceptance in the aging and the changes. I'm surrounded by older family members who are beautiful both inside and out. I've asked them, "Damn, how do you still look so good and who's your surgeon?" And although they have the same thoughts and insecurities about their own loss of youth, they remind me that you *can* age gracefully, and *then* they give me the name of their surgeon.

Maybe we all need to sit with who we are skin deep and find acceptance just like we do in every other area of our life.

With age comes wisdom and of course, some regrets. For all of you young women reading this, I can't stress enough how important it is to appreciate every single thing about yourself now. Maybe it's the texture and thickness of your hair, the tautness of your skin, the fullness of your lips, the flexibility of your body, the energy, and stamina to run 5 miles or stay up all night dancing. The things you take for granted now will be the very things you look back on one day and wish you still had or felt good enough to do.

I was cleaning off a hard drive one night and found old pictures of myself from a trip to Cancun with my family. I was wearing a green Hawaiian print bikini and I marveled at how smooth and tight my skin was. My belly button was still halfway up my torso where it started before I had kids complete with a sexy little belly button ring.

But you know what I remember from that time in my life? I thought I was old and fat. At 31 years old, I felt old. And at 105 pounds, I felt fat. Let that sink in for a moment.

My sister encouraged me to enter the Miss Solaris bathing suit competition because I had won the title 8 years earlier but the only thought I had at the time was, "I'm too old for this and I'll embarrass myself if I enter."

I entered anyway because my family was egging me on and besides, I was in Mexico. These people didn't know me so what did I have to lose? I went out there, let go of my concerns that people would be judging me, danced my booty off and just had fun. And this "old fat" 31-year-old took 3rd place. Not a bad showing for someone who thought everyone was judging her.

My point is, do *all the things*. Appreciate the things about yourself at every age. Appreciate how you look and how you feel. Be present to the privilege of being young and be present to the privilege of aging. Both come with insecurities, but insecurity is a natural part of being human. Instead of running away from it, maybe we ask ourselves, **what can it teach us?**

When I'm feeling insecure about anything, I sit with it and go deeper. I ask the question, "Will this feeling matter a year from now? Who am I trying to be in this moment that isn't aligned with the truth?"

Usually, I'm insecure because I'm trying to be something I'm not. When I was younger, I was trying to look a certain way and that way wasn't me. A short athletic girl can't expect herself to look like a six-foot Victoria Secret model.

Sometimes I tried to be a person I wasn't. Most of the time that was at a job where I was being asked to be more of something that didn't feel natural to me. More "corporate", more conservative, less empathetic, less of myself.

As I've gotten older the insecurities are teaching me to appreciate what I do have, and not what I don't. Who cares about the lines on my face, when my body is healthy and can do things my own parents no longer can? Why focus on my looks when I have a working brain that still solves problems, manages a full-time job, parenting young kids and is constantly coming up with new ideas?

My point is, we can be present to the thoughts and feelings we have around aging, but at the end of the day, we aren't taking our bodies with us. The only thing we leave with is our souls. *What is your soul meant to do while it's here on this earth and can you shift your thoughts to that purpose in those moments you feel insecure?*

Because we're here for *that*.

Our souls are here to push past the superficial things and remember why we're here and what we're meant to do. For me, I can accept I don't always love the aging process, but I also acknowledge I've got a bigger purpose in this world, and I'm not done yet.

What's your something bigger? Why are you here?

Back away from the mirror, from scrolling your Instagram feed, from comparing yourself to someone else and get present to that.

In the moments I'm fully present to that, what I see reflected back at me in the mirror is Divine beauty and grace. And for that, I'm grateful. Even if I still don't understand what the hell is happening to my face.

Dina Strada

Chapter 5
Boundaries Are Your Bestie

If I'm honest, boundaries are something I've struggled with most of my life. They require me to love myself enough in that moment to override any fear I'm having of upsetting or disappointing another person.

Self-love requires boundaries. Ironclad, consistent, strong boundaries. Without them, our lives can feel out of control, overwhelming and filled with resentment.

But let's admit setting boundaries is hard. Most of us want to be liked. We want to show the world we can do everything, be everything and not complain about it. We don't want to let people down. We don't want to upset family members and friends. Maybe some of us grew up in families with no boundaries so we're not even sure what one looks like.

In addition to hitting the jackpot with friends, I've won the Mega Millions when it comes to family. My family is the best. And as much as I love my family, I should mention we *are* Italian, and the Italians don't know the meaning of the word boundaries! We live to be involved in every part of your life. It's just our thing.

Of course, this does have its advantages. Since we all know what's going on in everyone's lives, there really aren't any secrets. And there is always someone there to support you because there's no hiding what you're going through.

Marriage on the rocks? Trust me, we know all about it! And even though we try not to gossip, everyone will be talking about what you should and shouldn't do. It's the Italian way.

Financial problems? We may not know how deep in debt you are but trust me, we know there's trouble brewing and we're saying novenas that God sends help soon.

Trying to get pregnant but don't want anyone knowing? Oh gurl...We all know you're doing the deed with the hubs every chance you get and are making even more novenas that you get knocked up soon!

Anyway, I digress. The point is, even though culturally my family boundaries were harder to put in place because we're a very tight knit bunch, I had to learn over the years how to be better about setting my own boundaries.

WHAT THE HECK DO YOU MEAN BY BOUNDARIES?

I don't want to assume everyone knows what I mean when I say, "set a boundary". Setting boundaries is a form of self-care. It helps create a clear guideline/rule/limit of how you want to be treated and what is and isn't acceptable to you.

Boundaries are a way we honor our need to feel safe and respected.

Got it? Fabulous.

Here's the single most important truth about how we are treated in the world by others... *We teach people how to treat us. And we do this by the boundaries we set with others.*

When we don't like someone's behavior and don't speak up in the moment, we've sent the message that acting that way is OK. Why would they think anything different? We haven't told them that canceling plans at the last minute or giving us unsolicited advice on how to parent our kids pisses us off, so they keep doing it and then we wonder why they don't understand how hurtful it is to us.

They don't understand or even know it's hurtful because we've allowed them to do it over and over again. We haven't set any boundaries around it.

Never have I seen this happen more often than in romantic relationships. I can't tell you how many friends and clients I work with who will complain about the same thing over and over again and when I ask the question, "Have you told them how this makes you feel?" their response is, "Well, no. They should just know it makes me feel shitty."

Well, no, they probably don't know. As crazy as that may sound when it should be obvious. Or maybe they do but because you don't say anything, they think their shitty behavior is OK and know you'll continue to stick around and put up with it because you've been putting up with it so far.

So, if you want something to be different, you need to pull up your big girl panties (or big boy boxers) and step up your boundary game.

WHAT WEAK/NO BOUNDARIES LOOK LIKE

If you're wondering whether the boundaries in your own life are weak, these are some tell-tale signs:

- You take responsibility for other people's emotions and reactions.
- You often find yourself giving in to someone even when it's not what you want.
- You say yes when you mean no.
- You struggle to tell others how you feel.
- You don't speak up for yourself.
- You often feel taken advantage of.
- You find yourself doing things you don't want to do.

If your kids are running your household, you have weak boundaries.

If you feel that a friend will get mad at you when you say you can't do something for them, you probably have weak boundaries.
If you're constantly over-extended and continue to say yes to people and take on more than you can handle you have weak boundaries.

And when our boundaries are weak, we aren't honoring ourselves.

WHY MOST OF MY
ROMANTIC RELATIONSHIPS TANKED

I'll share some of my relationship history post-divorce because when I was married, I knew how to speak up for myself. Once I was let loose in the dating pool, I had to relearn the rules and that it was OK to say no to things.

Like most women after a breakup, my ego was shattered and so was my self-esteem. Even though I knew the ending of my marriage was the best thing for both of us I still felt rejected. I hadn't dated since the pre-Bumble, Hinge, Tinder, OK Cupid days when guys didn't have a smorgasbord of hot women to swipe from 24-7.

I mean, I just didn't know what I was up against.

Anyway, I didn't really even need to put myself out there because I found there were lots of guys I already knew or met through friends who wanted to date me. And although I was flattered, I wasn't ready. In fact, I was kind of a shit show and had no business dating anybody. But still, I wanted to stay open and who was I to turn down a hot guy who liked me?

A few things happened that I'm embarrassed to admit but I want to share it because I know I'm not the only woman who has made these mistakes.

I was at an event one night and met a guy I had a great connection with and spent a lot of time with. It got late and everyone was crashing on the floor for the night, and he found me in the living room and came and laid next to me. He was a nice guy, cute and attentive. When I first meet someone, even though I may be attracted to them and feel a connection, I still need time to get to know them better before I allow anything physical to happen.

But it was very early in my newly single days, and I didn't know how to speak up and set boundaries. So, when he laid next to me and started kissing me, I thought it was innocent enough and didn't push him away. When he started touching me (and he *did* ask first if that was OK before he laid a hand on me), I didn't want to hurt his feelings or offend him, so I didn't say no even though I didn't feel comfortable.

Anyway, nothing else happened that night, but I left feely icky and embarrassed. I wasn't ready for anybody to physically touch me, but I kept blaming myself. I didn't say no. I didn't speak up. I was ashamed at my lack of boundaries that I told no one what had happened.

And women do this all the time. We relent or give in to being sexual or intimate before we're ready or when we don't want to. Some of us have sex too soon without knowing what the relationship is yet and then feel hurt when we're told, "I don't want to be exclusive" or "I want something casual."

These are examples of weak boundaries and for a period of time in my life, I was the Queen of the Weak. What I've learned over time is that not speaking up and having what is often an uncomfortable conversation with someone I don't want to be with is not honoring myself or the other person.

More recently I've had trouble being honest that I don't want to spend time with someone who I could sense wanted more from me than I was willing to give. This hasn't just been in romantic relationships. We all have people who we just don't vibe with, or don't like enough to want to hang out with. They may be perfectly nice people, but they just aren't *our* people.

I don't know about you, but I'm chronically polite and don't want to hurt anyone's feelings. So, when they say, "Hey, if you ever want to grab a drink," or "Why don't you come over and we can hang out," I've been a total shit, plastered a smile on my face and eked out an, "Ah... OK. Sounds fun," when it was the last thing I wanted to do.

No! Whhhhhhyyyyyy??? I don't wanna! I don't know why I still struggle with the boundary setting. It doesn't have to be a blow off. But we do have to be direct.

Today, my boundaries are better but still not perfect. I worry a little less about hurting someone's feelings, and when it comes to dating, I don't put myself in situations where I'll be alone with someone I'm not sure about. I find ways to work my boundary into casual conversations with men so they're clear up front what I'm comfortable with and what I'm not.

Personal boundaries are hard, but setting boundaries in the workplace can be even harder. Especially if you're a people pleaser.

When I first started out in my career, I wanted to be that people pleasing, ass-kissing rock star I was in school. I had career goals, and I was going to do whatever it took to prove myself to achieve them.

When we're in an entry level position, just starting out in our careers, we need to be willing to pay our dues. Sometimes that means long hours, lower pay and being grateful for the opportunity. But once we've proven ourselves and shown our commitment to the job, we have a right to ask for more of what we want. And we *always* have the right to be treated fairly and with respect.

I've been fortunate throughout my career to work at great companies with incredible people. I haven't experienced some of the horror stories friends of mine have been through (*Succession* fans, let's not forget the "Bore on the Floor" episode). But I didn't know how to set boundaries with my time or the hours I worked. I was afraid to speak up when the workload was too much. Hell, I still struggle with this.

Setting boundaries at work is everything. You can still be a hard worker and highly productive even if you don't respond to emails at 11:00 at night. You can take a sick day when you're sick to take care of yourself. You're allowed to take vacation time that you've accrued.

Remember, we teach people how to treat us. If you train your boss that she or he can call, text, or email you at any hour of the day and you'll always respond or agree to take on more work than you can handle, you haven't established any boundaries. And if we haven't established any boundaries at work, we can expect to feel burnt out, frustrated, and miserable most of the time.

Again, boundaries are your bestie.

"I'M NOT A GOOD WIFE, MOTHER, FRIEND, DAUGHTER, SON, ETC. IF I DON'T PUT THEM FIRST"

Lastly, can we just talk about the boundaries with our family and friends?

Putting those people first because we love them is typical, especially when it comes to our family. We want to make the people we love happy. We don't want to upset them or let them down. Family is family and most of us want to do whatever we can to be there for those we love most.

We also need to honor our own boundaries by taking care of ourselves first. And this can be a tricky balance.

I have found for myself, I say yes to almost everything, even when I don't want to do it out of a sense of responsibility. For me, saying no feels selfish. My parents are both very giving and selfless people, so they are the role models I look up to. They have always been there for me and for my children and I want to emulate them and be giving of my own time and support. Learning to find the balance and do what's best for me has taken lots and lots of practice and I still have yet to master it. But like any practice, the more I do it, the easier it gets.

Here's what I've found works best ~ total honesty.

For example, as I've gotten older and my plate has gotten more full, I find I don't want to make as many plans on the weekends. I want to sit around in my yoga pants, unshowered, makeup-less and binge watch Netflix or read a good book. I know, I sound like a raging good time, don't I?

When I was younger and afraid that my saying no would upset someone, I'd agree to plans I had zero interest in doing out of guilt only to feel resentful and angry at myself later. Now I'm honest with friends if they invite me somewhere and I don't want to go. "Wow, that sounds so fun, but I've had a crazy week and I blocked that night off for a little me time. I'm planning to be in my pajamas by 9pm but have a drink for me!"

Believe me, they don't care, and they don't take it personally. In fact, some of them wish they thought of doing it themselves!

When my kids want me to drive them somewhere and I've been running all day and doing one more drive across town is going to set me over the edge, I don't agree to it anymore and complain later. I've learned to say, "I wish I could take you now, but I've got too much on my plate today. Maybe you can get a ride or do this another day?"

And you know what? My kids don't argue or think I'm a crappy mom. Ninety-nine percent of the time when I say no to something, their response is, "No problem mom." They may be disappointed, but they understand I would do it in a heartbeat if I had the time and I'm saying no because I can't.

The stronger my boundaries have gotten with those closest to me, the happier and more relaxed I've become and the more empowered I feel. Taking care of our own emotional needs is as important as taking care of a small child. If we don't do it, nobody else will.

As for us Italians, we respect your whole boundary thing if you insist on them, but don't expect us to at least try to get around them every once in a while. It's just who we are. At least that's the excuse I'm going to use with my own kids one day so I can stay all up in their business like a true Italian momma!

Chapter 6
Karma -
The Good, The Bad, and The Ugly

If I'm honest, one of the biggest motivators that stops me from doing shitty things to other people is knowing that shitty thing will find its way right back to me.

Trust me, I speak from experience.

I grew up Catholic. If you're Catholic, you know what that entails. Guilt, shame, more guilt, and shame, but at the end of the day if you're good enough you get to go to Heaven and that's a huge motivator for us Catholics to be good people.

Anyhoo, I grew up being the "good girl. I cared so much about what everyone else thought of me to think about being bad. That doesn't mean I didn't do bad things. I participated in my share of lying to my parents, beating on my brother, talking behind a friend's back, even stealing a pair of earrings from Claire's boutique in the Seaview Square Mall when I was 15 years old just to see if I could get away with it (I did)!

But then I didn't... Because see, us Catholics are taught that God is always watching us. And God was watching that day. So just to remind me I didn't get away with anything, about a week later, I returned to my gym locker where I had left all my cool new clothes I had just bought from Merry-Go-Round at the same Mall I lifted the earrings from along with a beautiful tri-colored gold bracelet my boyfriend had given me for Christmas only to find...

Someone had broken into it and stolen all my stuff.

I couldn't believe it. I had never felt so violated. But in the same 60 seconds it took me to register what happened, my 15-year-old brain also registered the word, "KARMA", even though I didn't yet know what that word even meant.

Karma is a Sanskrit word that denotes the cycle of cause and effect, meaning each action a person takes in life will affect him or her at some point in the future.

This rule also applies to a person's thoughts and words. I like to think of it as perfect architecture. Once you throw a stone, it must fall down some time, somewhere.

As I got older, I began to notice how everything I had done in my entire life, both positive and negative, was coming back to me in some way. If I found myself on the receiving end of a thoughtful kind gesture from a friend, I recognized that I was receiving what I gave in my friendships. When someone lashed out at me unfairly and I felt like I had been punched in the gut, I felt in that moment as if God was holding a mirror up for me to look into, showing me the exact time and place I had made another person feel like that by lashing out at them.

I'll admit I was self-righteous over the years, judging another person for something they did while saying, "I'd never do that!" only to find myself at some point in the future doing that very same thing. And when I found myself doing that thing I'd think, "I can't believe I judged that person for doing what I just did. I'm not a bad person and I just made the same choice."

Oh, now I get it. Things aren't so black and white.

There's the grey. Grey is when we lie to avoid a confrontation or hurting somebody's feelings. Grey is giving into our kids because we're too damn exhausted to fight them after we judged another mom for giving into theirs. Grey is when we gossip about another friend's marriage, then feel hurt when we find out a friend is talking about ours. Let's admit, we all do crappy things. It doesn't mean we're bad people.

I once believed that Karma was a bad thing. As in the old adage, "Karma will get you".

What I've come to realize is that karma is the Universe giving us the opportunity to experience all sides of a situation to teach us compassion. If we haven't walked in another's shoes, how can we understand what they're going through? How can we *really* say we'd never do something if we've never been in those same circumstances and don't know what we'd actually do?

If we haven't been betrayed, how can we understand what betraying another human being feels like to them? If we've never been a boss with a ton of responsibility to manage, how can we understand how difficult it might be day to day to manage people and make them happy? If we've never been depressed, broke, single, married, childless, a parent, abused, in love with two people at once, ghosted, lost a parent or someone we love... we can't say we would "never feel that way" or "never act like that" or any of the other assumptions we make about people and their decisions when we've never walked a day in their shoes.

I used to act like a complete BI-ATCH to my own mother at times growing up when all she was trying to do was love me and give advice to help me. A few times when I really hurt her she'd say, "Wait one day until you have kids. You'll understand."

Flash forward years later when my son and daughter started rolling their eyes at me and I worried incessantly about them every time they walked out the door the way my mother worried about us. I've called her more than once over the last few years and said "OMG now I get it. I've become YOU!" We'd have a good laugh and I'd apologize and tell her how much I appreciate everything she did for us and still does to this day. Because until I was a mother myself, I just didn't get it. I mean, how can you get anything until you're in the same sitch? My sister and I often look at each other when one of our girls is screaming or mouthing off and nod in agreement, "Karma... mom wished it on us!"

On the flip side, let's admit that often someone we know who has done us dirty gets their comeuppance and God is being good to us that day and directs that tidbit of info our way so we hear about it. #karma

That's how I see karma working in my own life. It's been a teacher. It allows me to see and feel how my words, actions and inaction affect others. It's taught me to go back to people in my life I've hurt and take responsibility for where I was wrong when I've had greater perspective on how they must have felt rather than being so focused on my own feelings.

It's allowed me to forgive. I can't count how many times I've judged someone for some injustice they committed to me, only to do the very same thing to someone else. We're human and we make mistakes. We all screw up at times. I find that showing ourselves and other people some grace in those moments really can make a difference.

I believe most people are doing the very best they can at the moment. Sometimes our best sucks and we behave like complete assholes. I don't know about you, but I want my sucky moments to be forgiven which means I've got to be willing to do my own work and accept that other people also deserve to be forgiven.

So, going back to the Catholic thing, I have to admit... there is some truth that God is always watching. For those of you who aren't religious, let's just call it the Karma Gods. Every action in our life returns to us in some way to balance the scales. So be mindful of what you put out into the world every day. Can you imagine how different our world would be if we all put out only what we wanted to receive back and experience? I'd call that some big #karmagoals

Dina Strada

Chapter 7
We Teach People How to Treat Us

If I'm honest, it took me close to 44 years before I learned that I alone set the bar for how I'm treated in all my relationships. If someone is treating me poorly, I have nobody to blame but myself.

There's a term I became very familiar with not long after my divorce. It's called "breadcrumbing".

If you've never heard it, breadcrumbing is when we take something less than we want and deserve. In relationships, it's when someone gives us *just enough* time and attention to keep us interested but it still falls way short of what we want.

Breadcrumbing happens in all relationships including friendships. But romantic relationships (or at least those we want to be romantic) seem to be the place where most people experience the majority of breadcrumbing.

I can't say I was ever one of those women who desperately wanted or needed to be in a relationship. I can take it or leave it. At this moment in time, I don't want nor need to be in one which is very freeing. But for many of us, when we're in a vulnerable place, and not feeling particularly great about ourselves, it's the perfect breeding ground for someone to take advantage of us. Because let's face it, most of us will take whatever we can get when we're really into someone and simultaneously don't feel good about ourselves.

After my divorce, I found myself in several situations where I wanted a little more than I was getting but didn't say anything because I was afraid I'd come across needy and wasn't willing to let go of the little bit I *was* getting. My silence taught these men certain things were perfectly Ok with me, when in fact, they were NOT OK.

A couple of things I allowed that I wasn't OK with:

Leading me on or telling me how much they thought about me and wanted to spend time with me, then not following through.

Texting when they wanted to "get together and hang out" aka... fool around with me, but with no strings attached.

Sporadic communication that made me bat shit crazy wondering if they were into me at all, then once I gave up on them, they'd rope me in again with some flirty texting followed by another round of crickets.

Being an all-around asshole.

I didn't speak up and communicate that their behavior didn't make me feel good or left me confused about what they wanted. I wanted to be "the cool chick" so I rolled with things to make them (and myself) believe I didn't need much.

In the meantime, I would vent and complain to my closest friends. "What's up with him? How long do I have to put up with this shit?"

My best friend Elizabeth would say, "Until you love yourself enough to not accept it anymore."

Oof.

I thought I loved myself plenty. I think most of us think we love ourselves and wouldn't allow someone to jerk us around. But the truth is, when we care about someone or are in love and think we're not worthy of something better, we'll take whatever breadcrumbs are thrown our way which leaves the other person thinking we're perfectly happy. Why would they offer us a whole loaf of bread if we're not asking for it? This kind of goes back to the old saying, "why buy the cow when you're getting the milk for free?"

What I started to learn the hard way was that I'm 100% responsible for how people treat me.
Not eighty percent.
Not ninety-nine percent.
One hundred percent.

So, I stopped my bitching.

At any time, I could walk away and say, "No thanks." or "You know what, this isn't really working for me. I want x and you want y, so I think we're just not in the same place right now." No harm. No foul. Nobody has to be the bad guy.

You don't like the fact that your spouse or best friend always runs late? Well, they have no reason to change their behavior if you do nothing but scream at them when they turn up late over and over again. It's like hearing the teacher from Charlie Brown. "WA WA WA WA... WAAAAA!" Actually, attach a consequence to them being late (like leaving the place you were supposed to meet up 20 minutes ago) and you might see some different behavior.

Maybe you're in one of those, "I have no idea what I'm doing with this person" *situations* but you keep allowing the *situation* to go on for months not understanding why you're in it at all. In the meantime, you're calling every friend to weep dramatically into the phone about what a jerk he is and how pathetic you are for putting up with it but never do anything about it. My friend Jules is doing this right now but afraid to speak up and ask the guy what they are. It's driving her batty.

Yea, I get ya sister. Been there. Done that. You're teaching him how to treat you.

Years ago, I was in a *thing* with this guy. I'd call it dating, but I think the word dating would have freaked him out, so we referred to what we were doing as *hanging out.* I guess you could label this thing we were in as *friends with benefits* although we had more than friend feelings for each other. We were in a *thing,* call it what you want.

He was a breadcrumber. Hot, then cold. Cold than hot. I never knew day to day, week to week what guy would show up that day or what to expect from him. And because there were no promises made, I felt I deserved just breadcrumbs even though it left me unsatisfied and a little taken advantage of. It was a relationship where he set the rules, he decided when and if we'd hang out and he called the shots. I'm embarrassed even admitting this.

This didn't align with who I was; a confident, independent, I've got-my-shit-together woman who valued and respected myself. I wanted and deserved more but deep down knew he wasn't the guy. But I'll be honest, I taught him it was OK to treat me like that.

How did I do that?

For one, I never asked for more.

I jumped when he called and rearranged my schedule when he wanted to hang out. I pretended I didn't care about him as much as I did. I didn't speak up when he canceled plans at the last minute or tell him how much it hurt my feelings when he made me feel like I was an option rather than a priority.

And like most of us have done at one point or another at some point in our lives, I allowed him to make me feel like shit. I mean, seriously. I knew I was worth more than that.

So, one night we had plans to *hang out.* I had rearranged my schedule that week to make the night work for him, something I had done often. I was sitting at lunch with a friend just a few hours before we were scheduled to meet up, my overnight bag already packed in my car, arrangements made with my ex to take the kids for the night when I heard my phone vibrate...

"Hey, gotta cancel tonight."

I don't think he gave me a reason which was standard behavior for him, so I know he thought nothing of it. Better plans probably came up or he just wasn't feeling that day like he wanted to see me. Didn't matter. I had almost gotten used to the last-minute cancellations when something better came up. But this time... this time was different. *I wasn't playing anymore.*

I turned the phone over on the table and tried to pretend I was still listening to my lunch companion as my heart pounded wildly in my chest working its way up to my ears, drowning out the sound. For 30 seconds all I could see was red. It felt like rage, but quickly it simmered down and diffused into the most amazing feeling ever.

Peace. I actually felt at peace. Because I knew I was finally done.

I didn't respond to him. I didn't yell or scream or tell him off. I saw no point in putting any more energy into the "situation". I simply decided at that moment I would no longer be just an option.

We weren't just friends with benefits. We were actual friends. I really enjoyed and loved our friendship, but I was willing to let go of both to take care of myself. I cut off the whole relationship with no explanation, Nada. I didn't return calls. I didn't respond to texts. I held my ground and didn't cave when I missed him or second guessed whether I had been too harsh.

I held my ground.

And let me tell you something...That was really hard. I was *devastated* over losing him. I missed his friendship and him in my life more than I ever thought possible.

And yet I had to make the hard choice. I chose myself.

I cried for months over him but was too embarrassed to tell anyone I was even upset so I didn't talk about it with anyone. I don't think I realized how much I cared about him or how important he was to me until I cut things off. It was the first time in years I respected myself enough to say, "This isn't what I want or how I deserve to be treated and I won't allow it."

I think it was maybe 3 years later that we reconnected. We were both in a different place. The cutting off of the friendship and the *situation* had taught us both a lot about ourselves. He told me later he had done a lot of soul searching after that day and realized his behavior, which was a pattern that showed up with most women, was wrong, immature, and shitty. I admitted I should have been clearer about what I was looking for and communicated better rather than just going with the flow of what *he* wanted.

And from *that* place... The way I wanted to be treated was born. The two of us are great friends now. No benefits and no bullshit. He has treated me with integrity, respect, and honesty since I've allowed him back in my life. He shows up consistently as a friend and I don't believe that would have ever happened had I not been willing to walk away when he wasn't.

We teach people how to treat us.

We teach our friends and our parents and our children how to treat us. We teach our business partner, our employees, our boss and even the dog how to treat us. The way we show up in those relationships mirrors for them what we're willing to put up with, how they speak to us and what's acceptable behavior.

We don't have to be a jerk to set boundaries with others. We *do* have to be consistent and clear what it is we need and be honest with ourselves whether another person is able to give that to us.

And if they're not... *bye Felicia!*

As difficult as it is, we need to be willing to let some people go who can't or won't treat us in a way we feel is respectful. We can't be afraid to walk away from relationships when the other person can't or won't give us what we want. We don't need to be victims in these scenarios. I've walked away from plenty of relationships disappointed but always more self-aware of where I played a part in accepting something that wasn't aligned with who I am and where I still need to do some work around self-love and boundaries.

Since that particular relationship, I have not been in another one like it. I've never faltered or gone backwards. I've had other men come in and pull the same kind of *hey I'm hot, Oh wait...now I'm cold* behavior, but I don't engage anymore. Even when they're smokin' hot! Even when I want to lick those breadcrumbs off their hot sexy abs. I still resist. I have good friends who remind me, "Oh girl, he's waving a red flag. Reminds me of FRIENDS WITH BENEFITS GUY. Back away pronto!"

So, I back away. I've learned that accepting anything less than I want is not just unfair to me, but to the other person too. Which has made it very easy to be consistent.

Today, I can say there isn't one person in my life who doesn't treat me in a way that feels good. It's become a practice to run from anything that even slightly resembles a "situation" with a red flag waving in front of it. Heed the red flag ladies! They're always a warning that you can do better.

Chapter 8
I Wasn't a Natural at This Parenting Thing

If I'm honest, I have days when I feel ill equipped to parent. Maybe it's just me, but there are days I want my kids to parent me. I want them to come up with a dinner menu for the week, do the laundry, make the hard decisions, or just hold me and tell me everything's gonna be alright.

I was not a natural when it came to this mothering thing.

It probably didn't help that my first born had colic (or was sent from Hell to torture me). He cried non-stop at least 19 hours a day and I'm not exaggerating when I say that. I spent most of those first few months exhausted, delirious and in tears, counting the days until my maternity leave would be over so I could go back to work.

The thought of going back to the office felt like the equivalent of a relaxing day at the spa where I only had to be someone else's bitch for 8 hours a day instead of 24. Plus, they let me go to the bathroom when I wanted, and I got to eat my lunch sitting down which I didn't realize was a perk until I had a baby.

My brother was the only one at that time who had a kid and I used to call him regularly to ask stupid questions like "How do I figure out this swaddle blanket?" "Why does he pee through his diaper every day?" and "Is green poop normal?" My brother would tell me these questions were what Google was for and hang up on me.

From that day on, at least for the first 3-4 years, I struggled being a mother. Since I don't want my first born to end up in therapy after he reads this, I want to make it clear that I don't blame him for my struggles. Becoming a parent for the first time is a huge adjustment for anyone. Unless you're one of those annoying people who brag, "Oh, *when I had a baby, everything came so naturally for me!*" Medals are to the left...

But if any of you mommas are like me and had or are having a hard time, I hope my story makes you feel better because literally I *sucked ass* when my first kid was born.

In addition to the fact that he didn't sleep through the night until he was 4 years old and by *didn't sleep through the night* I mean screamed nonstop at the top of his lungs for hours on end, thrashed about in his crib/toddler bed like he was being murdered by some unseen entity and threw epic tantrums that would make Linda Blair in *The Exorcist* look like the Blessed Mother.

He was hard. The whole thing was just hard. The only time I slept was if I slipped out in the middle of the night and went to my friend Danica's condo next door to drown out his screams or after we moved into our new house, snuck into the closet under the stairwell.

My ex was the rock and the only reason I made it through that time in my life. My son loved him to pieces and the two of them bonded even through the tantrums. He was the calm, patient voice of reassurance that we would make it through this season of hell at a time when I was falling apart.

Then came my daughter. And since God does not give us more than we can handle we were blessed with a quiet, content, happy little angel baby.

She timed sleeping through the night to coordinate with the exact day I was scheduled to go back to work. She cried only when she was hungry or wet. And other than giving me a dirty look when I won't let her watch the *Real Housewives of New Jersey* with me, she's thrown very few tantrums in her life except for the time period she was so clingy we couldn't put her down for 5 minutes. Wait, maybe that was just last week.

Anyhoo, 4 months after she was born, and because God has a sense of humor and thought I could handle more since he did just give me a good baby, my ex-husband moved out (details which I won't divulge here out of respect for my kids), and I became a single parent. Out in LA with my family 3000 miles away in NJ, parenting two young kids, one who was just 4 months old, and one who had just turned 4 (and barely slept through the night) well, let's just say that wasn't the easiest time in my life.

Ok, full transparency...it sucked. It was the worst time of my life, and I was an epic shit show. I can't wrap this one up in a pretty bow.

I was trying to just get through the days while grieving the loss of my marriage and best friend. Let's face it, parenting is hard enough if you're lucky enough to have a partner to do it with. Parenting solo is a different kind of challenge. But this is about parenting in general, whether you're doing it with a partner or completely on your own.

We are incredibly hard on ourselves as parents. I think we all go into parenthood with these grand illusions of how blissful, fulfilling and rewarding it's going to be and then are surprised to find it's not at all what we thought it would be.

Maybe we had grandiose ideas that we'd be that mom or dad who makes organic meals for our kids, dresses them impeccably every day, sends them off to school with their teeth brushed and flossed to perfection, their hair styled in cute French braids or a cool spiked do.

We planned to volunteer in the classroom reading books or become the class mom organizing field trips and school parties. We imagined we'd only ever talk to them in a calm, reasonable voice at all times and go to bed each day with a sense of accomplishment because our kids are peacefully sleeping in their own beds after saying their prayers at 8pm sharp.

Then we find ourselves at the fast-food drive-thru picking up chicken nuggets and fries for dinner on our way to soccer practice which we're late for again because our kid couldn't find his cleats which resulted in a 20-minute meltdown (ours).

Or we overslept because we were up until 1am the night before catching up on work that didn't get done that day because one of our kids had a 4-hour doctor's appointment in the middle of the afternoon. Plus a 10-page form which was at the bottom of their backpack needed to be filled out by this morning so they could attend a class trip and now we're late dropping them off at school and just noticed they have a big fat disgusting hole in the knee and OMFG is that crusted ketchup on their shirt from last Thursday's night dinner?? (Damn, did I forget to do laundry again)? Their teeth for sure haven't been brushed in at least 24 hours and we know this because our kid hasn't slept in their own bed since before the pandemic and we would have noticed if they had remembered to actually brush their teeth.

They didn't.

Volunteering is something you do maybe once a year out of guilt and includes you frantically running to the grocery store the night before to buy store bought cupcakes in one of those God-awful plastic containers with the frosting that's gonna turn their mouths neon blue for an entire week to send in for the class party.

And forget the calm, zen voice asking them nicely to please pick their clothes up off the floor for the 118th time or flush the toilet, or not spit on the bathroom mirror or leave their dirty dishes with 3-day old ice cream in their beds. You have now become *that parent.* The unhinged, unreasonable, crazy person screaming hysterically at them at a decibel so loud you're pretty sure your neighbors have called the police to report a homicide.

So, the question is, *should we be so hard on ourselves as parents?*

Yes and no.

Yes, I think we have to hold ourselves to a somewhat reasonably high standard because we're raising tiny humans who depend on us and are going to go out into the world and interact with other humans. It's an enormous responsibility and we can't phone it in.

But like any other job in life we have, we can't do it perfectly and we're going to make mistakes along the way. We're going to have bad days. Hell, we're going to have bad years where we want to give up because we feel we're missing the mark every day. Those are called *the teenage years*. But if we're doing the very best we can in the moment, that's all we can ask of ourselves. When we know better, we do better.

The part of me that says no, we shouldn't be so hard on ourselves is the one that believes if we don't show empathy and compassion for ourselves then we can never teach that to our children. If we can't be vulnerable at times with our kids, then we can't raise kids who know vulnerability is a strength, not a weakness and a way to get in touch with how they feel about things.

If we're constantly picking ourselves apart and putting ourselves down every time we make a mistake, they won't learn it's OK for them to make their own mistakes.

I know that each year, I've made just a tiny bit more progress as a parent. I've learned what the important things are to focus on and worry about versus what things are OK to ease up on and let go. I'm not as hard on myself as I once was and don't spend every day worrying that the life I'm giving them will land them in therapy one day (I *know* they'll be in therapy one day and good for them for doing their inner work)!

I still struggle with making decisions, but I know I'm doing the best I can in every moment. I try not to sweat the small stuff that doesn't matter; pee on the toilet seat, a C on their report card, whether they got 8 hours sleep and ate 4 servings of vegetables that day. Because really that *never* happens.

But the big stuff that's worth a certain amount of fretting, I've gotten better at over time. I don't make those decisions alone. I consult their dad, my own mom, my sister, my mom friends who are just a little bit ahead in the parenting game than me who had to make the hard decisions themselves and made it through to the other side who can offer words of wisdom.

Here are the big things I've learned are important:

Making sure they feel loved. When they walk in the room, do I make them feel like I'm happy to see them or am I so distracted they feel unseen?

Making sure they feel emotionally and physically safe.

Being empathetic when they tell me they're scared or nervous or angry about something even when I don't understand.

Repeatedly showing them that I will love them unconditionally and my love isn't dependent on how they behave, what they accomplish or whether I approve of everything they do.

Apologizing to them when I'm wrong and owning my stuff when I make a mistake.

Listening to them and really hearing what they're saying to me.

Telling them they can do anything and be anything they want if they believe in themselves.

Supporting their dreams, no matter what.

Pushing them outside their comfort zone.

Watching who they hang out with and when I don't trust someone is a good influence, intervening.

Reminding them often that I'm not perfect and don't have all the answers and figuring some things out together.

Momma, you got this. Dads, you got this. Parenting is a journey, not a destination. My parents are 79 and 91 years old as of the writing of this chapter and they are still parenting me and my 2 siblings, even though we're all grown up. The love and feeling of wanting the very best for our children never wanes, and as an adult, I can say that the big stuff is all the things my own parents did for me that at the end of the day truly mattered.

The rest of it is the small stuff. Let it go, and let your kids figure some of that out for themselves. And remember, you don't need to be a natural at this parenting thing. Say, "good for you" to all those amazing mommas telling you how natural it is for them, and then go pour yourself a glass of wine and hide in a closet somewhere. I'll be right there at my own house toasting you and wishing you Godspeed on your journey.

Dina Strada

Chapter 9
The Shame Monster

One of the most disempowering feelings any of us can feel is shame. If I'm honest, I think if we had the courage to share our shame with another person, it would lose all its power over us.

Recently I went into my church's parish to get something called a sponsor certificate which is required to be my niece's sponsor to receive the sacrament of Confirmation. For those who aren't Catholic, Confirmation is the 3rd sacrament children receive to be initiated into the church after baptism and First Communion.

I loved growing up with a faith in something. I've leaned on prayer and the teaching of the Catholic church to get through many challenges in my life and believe that my faith is what gives me strength and has helped me accept the things I know I can't change.

But still, I've had my issues with the Catholic church over the years and they revolve around the shame aspect that is ingrained in many of their teachings.

If you were raised Catholic, (or Jewish) you can probably relate to what we jokingly refer to as "Catholic guilt". You feel guilty if you miss Mass. You feel guilty if you have impure thoughts, yell at your kids, tell a white lie or commit any other sin (which is why we go to confession). And if, like me, you're divorced and didn't get the marriage annulled by the church, then you may as well wear a scarlet letter on your chest with a big 'ole "D".

DIVORCED. SHAME!

I haven't felt shame in a long time. I used to feel a lot of shame around my eating disorder back in the days when I was hiding it from those close to me and I still feel shame thinking about things I've said or done over the years that have hurt people. Even when we apologize and make amends, it can be difficult to not obsess over our mistakes or still feel that hot burning shame in the pit of our stomachs thinking back on a time in our life we aren't proud of. Or remembering something another person said to us that made us feel unworthy of love or forgiveness.

My divorce for some reason still carries shame for me. It was never what I wanted or pictured for my life and being a member of the Catholic Church, which teaches that marriage is a lifetime commitment brings that shame right up to the surface for me. Although I know the right thing for everyone involved was to let that marriage go, I sometimes think that because I couldn't make it work that there's something wrong with me and maybe people must think I'm incapable of holding onto a relationship. I know this isn't true but deep down, we all tell ourselves stories. Getting out of my marriage was freeing and an act of self-love but my shame won't allow me to tell that story.

When my sister asked me to be my niece's Godmother, we knew technically I wasn't in "good standing" with the church because I was divorced. So, we just didn't mention that little factoid to the priest. SHAME! LYING! But the Confirmation thing forced me to have to go in front of the priest at my parish and basically get a "report card" of my faithfulness as a Catholic and verify my good standing with the church.

Listen, I knew going in this was gonna be tricky. There was paperwork that needed to be filled out and one of the questions asked my marital status. I couldn't very well *lie* could I? Lying would be another sin to feel guilt and shame over. Besides, as I just confessed, I had failed to mention to the church once before of my divorced status so they wouldn't deny me the honor of being my niece's Godmother 13 years earlier.

So, I took my black pen, checked off the "Divorced" box, and hoped for the best. That's when the Shame Monster reared its ugly head.

I saw the Parish secretary get visibly uncomfortable as she read through my paperwork. This poor woman had to deliver the bad news and I knew exactly what she was going to say before she said it, *"So, there's a slight problem. I'm going to read to you the eligibility requirements to be a sponsor directly from the Catholic handbook."*

Oh God, the holy handbook! Here it comes.

Then the sound drowned out as I heard her read something about needing to be married in the Catholic church and since I wasn't married by a priest that made me ineligible, but being I was no longer married at all, I was basically not in good standing and SHIT OUTTA LUCK.

I know this sounds ridiculous but before the words were out of her mouth, I felt the hot flush of shame creeping up the back of my neck and tears pricking my eyeballs because I already knew how the church saw me. I thought I was over this shame thing, but I think when we feel shame over something, it never really goes away.

I walked out in tears. I realized I couldn't let go of the shame around my marriage falling apart.

Because there is a God (or at least I believe in one), a few hours later the parish secretary called me back to let me know she had taken pity on me, spoke to the priest and he had granted permission to give me the required sponsor certificate despite my divorce status. I said a silent prayer to God thanking him for the pardon and kicked that Shame Monster to the curb.

Buh-bye.

WHAT'S YOUR SHAME?

If there was one thing I had the power to do it would be to wave a magic wand and rid people of their shame. It's an ugly, disempowering feeling society can make us feel and with social media our shame can be magnified by a 1000 since there are now loads of people out there weighing in on how they feel about us.

We all feel shame over something. If you're human, you're carrying around shame. Maybe it's around your body, your sexuality, living in a tiny place, being messy, taking antidepressants, not having kids, being divorced, being single, having an abortion or some mistake you made years ago that you still feel bad about.

Shame can't exist without our own feelings feeding it. If we can make peace with our past choices no matter how poor they may have been or our present circumstances whatever they are, we can rid ourselves of shame.

When I shared with people that I was writing a chapter about shame, so many of them asked if they could share theirs with me. My friend Victoria said, "I've got a whole lotta that, I'd love to unload it if it helps other people."

Most of the men and women I talked to wanted to be free of the stories they were carrying around about themselves. There is something so liberating about getting it out and realizing nobody has this big, horrible reaction to the thing you've done or a truth about yourself. As people shared their stories with me, there wasn't one where my reaction was, "OMG, that's horrible!" Instead, I breathed a sigh of relief. "Wow, me too. I get that."

With their permission I'm sharing just a few of their stories. I hope in hearing them, you'll feel not so alone in yours.

"I've always been ashamed of my body. I've been overweight my whole life, dieting on and off for years and even when I was thinner, I still never felt thin enough. People would comment how great I looked when I lost the weight and then nobody would say a thing to me when I put it all back on, as if I should be ashamed of myself for letting myself go. I don't think people who don't struggle with their weight understand how depressing and awful it is to feel like everyone is constantly looking at you and judging you just for having a different body than them. It's not like I'm not trying. The weight of being 50-60 pounds more than I want is emotionally heavier than the physical weight I've ever carried around." ~ Lisa

"I was sexually assaulted when I was in college by someone I knew. It was stupid. I was stupid. I had gotten drunk and was high and he took advantage of that. I was so afraid to tell anyone because I felt I deserved it. If I had been more responsible and hadn't drank so much or allowed myself to be alone with him, maybe it wouldn't have happened. I think my father would have told me I had it coming to me if I ever told anyone, so I didn't say a word." ~ Karen

"I had an affair for over a year with someone I reconnected with from college on social media. I love my husband. He's an amazing partner and my best friend. It wasn't about not loving him. I was trying to figure out what the connection was between me, and this person and he ignited something in me sexually I didn't know was there. I think there were things I wanted to try sexually over the years that I was embarrassed to tell my husband because we've been together since we were 16 years old. I thought he'd think I was dirty or look at me differently. With this other person, I didn't have to worry about what he thought about me because we knew it would never be anything more than a physical relationship. I felt so guilty about what I was doing the entire time but exploring my sexuality outside my marriage was

helping it because I was opening up sexually with my husband and being more honest with him about what I wanted. It's been a few years since the affair ended and I still feel guilty every day." ~ Jucinda

"I had an abortion. I was raised Catholic, and my parents told me if I ever came home pregnant, they would disown me. I never told a single person, not even the person who got me pregnant." ` ~ Karly

"I've struggled with depression and anxiety for most of my life and have been on antidepressants and other medication for anxiety since I was in my early 20's. People who don't suffer from mental illness or chronic depression don't realize how debilitating it is just to get out of bed. I don't want to be like this. I didn't ask to feel this way. I've done all the things people tell you to do; meditation, talking to a therapist, exercise, keeping a gratitude journal, reading self-help books. They help a little, but my medication is what keeps me functioning and able to get out of bed. Some people don't understand and judge me for it but I'm learning to accept this is just who I am." ~ Nick

"It took me until I was 25 years old to come out to my family that I was gay. In Mexican families, it just isn't accepted. I grew up with a father who used words like faggot and queer when I was growing up and basically told us that he would never accept a son who was gay. I knew when I chose to finally come out, I'd lose my family and I did. Being queer and proud was hard at first because of the shame my father made me feel growing up but I'm damn proud of myself and I have an amazing support system in friends. Still, we don't live in a world where everyone accepts us for who we are. I just want to feel proud of who I am." ~ Carl

"Unfulfilled in my marriage, I thought it was only an unfulfilling sex life, so I had an affair. It lasted 10 years and was just sex. I thought that was the way to help keep me in the marriage. Unfortunately, I realized that I was unhappy in almost every aspect of my life (personally and in the marriage). Unfortunately, the guilt over the 10-year sexual *relationship slowly ate at me and I carried that shame for years until I decided to leave my marriage. My ex-husband of almost 20 years does not know about this affair and I hope he doesn't find out as it was not about him, it was about me. The shame has dissipated with the realization that I am now in a place to make better choices for myself and my future." ~ Alyssa*

"I screwed my way through my first two years of college, finally on my own, looking for love but not understanding sex did NOT equal love. They were all one-night stands. I married the first man who asked. He cheated on me from the get-go, even though he said he loved me. We divorced after 2.5 years. More shame: I failed AGAIN. My mother was kind enough to hold her "I told you so"s until I was more ready to hear them." ~ Alanna

"I still feel shame over the way I treated girls back in my younger years. I was immature and struggling with my self-esteem so I would date one girl while juggling another at the same time, sometimes three or four at once. I wasn't honest with them and told all of them I wasn't seeing anybody else. It wasn't about them not being enough for me. It was about nobody being enough for me and me trying to prove to myself I was lovable and desirable. It all blew up in my face one night. Two of the women met at a dinner that both of them were not supposed to be at and I was completely busted. It was a disaster. I really hurt them and still feel guilty over what I did because that was one of many times I played games with women and was dishonest. It was just the one time I got caught." ~ Peter

Here's what I have to say about all our stories... we are all flawed in some way. Nobody has a right to judge us, so we have to stop judging ourselves.

You're still a great friend even if you're overweight or don't love your body. You can be a wonderful human being and struggle with alcohol or drug addiction. You can do great things in the world even if you struggle with mental illness. You are still lovable if you lied or cheated. You are just as important as the person sitting next to you no matter what you do for work, how much money is in your bank account or where you live.

We aren't our mistakes or our choices. And if you're still carrying around some BS story about who you are, or some so-called horrible thing you did in your past, I hope you can let it go and realize that every one of us has a shame monster who lives within us. Allow yourself some grace and know that all of your mistakes, no matter how seemingly awful, serve a purpose and your job is to figure out what that is and then move on with your life.

As for my guilt and shame hang up with the Catholic Church, maybe I'll never fully let it go but I did finally sit down with our Parish priest to talk through my feelings around my divorce, and he was absolutely wonderful. I think just talking about what we've done and how we feel is the thing that can kick shame to the curb.

And then, we can just move on with our lives.

Section 2

Loving Others

Dina Strada

Chapter 10
You Don't Need to Be in a Relationship to be Happy

If I'm honest, the most at peace I've ever been in my life have been the years I haven't been in a relationship. It's been those times I've really shown up for myself and learned to do things I thought I could never do alone from fixing a toilet to being my own best friend.

I have an email list I've grown over the years with loyal readers. One reader is a guy named Cliff (*name changed to protect his privacy). He responds to almost every email I send and for that reason alone he gets a shout out. He shared this story with me last week,

"I went out with my friend to hear some music the other night, and I sat next to this gorgeous woman, and really enjoyed her company that evening. We had a real connection. When it was over, he thought I was crazy for not getting her phone number. I just didn't want to ruin something nice. It's a great feeling to sit and enjoy the things I enjoy without worrying about whether I should be sharing it with someone else. I have come to believe that if it's supposed to happen, it will. I'm tired of trying to make things happen."

I really want you to hear that last line because this insight he had about himself is so powerful. The more we force something to happen, the less likely it's going to happen.

I'm not suggesting you stop chasing after what you want. I've had friends who are complete messes after another relationship ended or one never even got off the ground argue with me that they don't want to be alone so why should they give up trying?

I don't think anyone should give up trying if being in a relationship is really what you want. But I do think not spending the time to get to know yourself, learning how to be alone, and not seeking validation from another person is an important piece of work to do before you jump into the search again.

Also, believing you can't be happy if you're not in a relationship is bullshit.

My friend shared this about her own journey coming to terms with the way she was chasing a relationship,

"I honestly felt at one time that if I wasn't with someone, people would think there was something wrong with me. I've never been married and most of my friends are coupled up. I put so much pressure on myself over the years to be with someone, anyone really... that I allowed myself to be breadcrumbed, emotionally abused, taken advantage of, and just unhappy in general just so I didn't have to be single again.

Finally, one day I was having dinner with this guy I had been dating on and off for about a year. He wasn't even what I wanted. I was physically attracted to him, but we had almost nothing in common and he didn't have any of the qualities in a long-term partner I was looking for anyway. I don't know why I stayed in it so long but months later I realized it was because I was scared to be alone. I thought to myself, 'who will I eat dinner with if I break up with him? Who will I watch TV with at night? What if I never meet someone else?' I was totally willing to settle so I didn't have to be alone."

I met a man recently who had just broken up with a guy he was seeing for months. He told me he was embarrassed to admit that sometimes he thinks he wants a relationship, but when he finds himself in one, he gets bored quickly and wants out. *"I don't know if I really want to be in something or I feel I'm supposed to be in something because everyone else is."*

I hear this from so many people. They don't even know if being in a relationship is what they truly want or if the pressure our society puts on us to be in one is what's driving them to be out there looking at all.

Here's what I've learned over the years... We have to know ourselves first. And I mean really know ourselves and what we want before we declare we "want a partner" or "we want to be in a relationship" when we're still figuring ourselves out.

We have to love our own company.

We need to learn how to forgive. We need to let go of the anger, hurt and resentment we might still be carrying over something that happened in our past with someone else before we can be in a relationship with another person without all that baggage.

We need to forgive our ex or forgive ourselves for what we did or didn't do in the past.

We have to love all the broken, messy, and not so beautiful parts of ourselves first before we go searching for someone else who inevitably we'll project all that shit onto.

We have to know how to take care of ourselves. This isn't somebody else's job. When I say take care of yourself, I mean financially, emotionally, spiritually, and physically.
- Do you know what you need to feel physically balanced, healthy, and good in your own skin?
- Do you know how to fill your own cup?
- Can you pay your own bills?
- Do you know how to comfort and be there for yourself when you've had a bad day?

Of course, a great partner will want to support us when we're struggling with something. But supporting us is very different from taking care of us or having to carry us. The heavy lift lies with us. In the years since my marriage ended, I've really learned how to take care of myself on every level. Although I was always incredibly independent and doing that long before I got married, like most people, I still leaned on my ex for certain things - from making hard decisions to doing the "manly" things I didn't want to deal with (most involving trash, technology and anything that needed to be assembled)!

If you're looking for a relationship to validate that you're "enough", or special, or because you want someone to take care of you, you'll never find what you're looking for. Nobody can give that to you. Nobody but you.

You don't need to be in a relationship to feel special. You're not less than other people because you've been single for 10 or 15 or even 20 years. People don't think you're a loser. In fact, most people don't think about your relationship status much at all (except maybe your mom). So, stop focusing on it.

It may sound cliche to say, but when you're doing you, when you love yourself, when you find peace being with yourself, you'll find you don't need a relationship at all. It doesn't mean you won't want one or desire to have a partner to share your life with. It simply means you won't be chasing it the way I see so many people chasing one now because they tie their self-worth into whether another person wants to be with them.

My best friend Elizabeth once told me when I really loved myself, I wouldn't settle for anything less than what I wanted, and I wouldn't take it personally when someone I was interested in wasn't interested in me. She was absolutely right.

The truth is I didn't learn to love myself until I was completely alone. I didn't do the deep soul searching or the hard work of healing from past hurts, disappointments, unhealthy habits, and behaviors until I was forced to sit with myself without the distraction of being with another person telling me what to do and how to do it.

You don't need a relationship to be happy. You really don't. Let go of that thought today if you're serious about being happy.

Work on falling in love with yourself instead and I promise the rest will fall into place without you having to work so hard for it.

Dina Strada

Chapter 11
What Love Should Feel Like

If I'm honest, it's been so long since I've been in love that I sometimes forget what it feels like, but not enough to remember that love should never feel like you're losing yourself.

My first love, who I met when I was 16 years old, is the embodiment of what I believe love should feel like.

Chris and I fell in love during our junior year in high-school and stayed together until I left for Boston College. Although our lives went in vastly different directions, we have still managed to stay in touch and be a part of each other's lives for over 30 years. He's always the first person to wish me a happy birthday on Sept 11th *every single year* and still makes me feel as special as he did when we were kids.

Over those 30 plus years as we both fell in love with other people, got married and built our separate lives, we continued to check in with each other every so often to share what was going on and talk about our struggles. He has always been supportive and encouraging no matter what I'm going through, and I try to do the same for him. But the one thing I reflect on when I think back on our relationship in high school is how Chris always made me feel and still does today.

Safe. Cherished. Accepted. Supported. Adored. Our love back then and now is based on loyalty and friendship.

I have been in love many times in my life and can admit now that I didn't always feel all these things in those relationships. We can love someone and not feel safe with them. We can be wildly in love with another person and not share a friendship. Someone can say they love us and still not truly accept us for who we are. I think if we all went back to our very first loves, which are typically full of innocence and firsts, free of past trauma, woundings and any agendas, we'd remember what real love is *supposed* to feel like.

Love feels safe. If you don't feel emotionally or physically safe, it's not love.

Love is about acceptance. Maybe you don't like your partner's messiness or their obsessive need to organize the refrigerator in neat rows with the larger items in the back and the labels all facing front, or the fact that they show up late to literally *everything* including your own wedding, but you accept them. You accept their weird idiosyncrasies and annoying habits. You make jokes about them. You tease each other. But both of you feel accepted by the other person.

Love doesn't feel confusing. There are no guessing games with each other, no wondering where you stand or how the other person feels about you or the important things in the life you share together. It's solid. It feels good, not volatile.

Love feels secure. You know this person has your back no matter what. They don't abandon you when life gets messy and complicated. They don't run away when you're having an argument or disagree. They don't make you feel the grass is greener somewhere else and you're lucky they stick around. They don't disappear. When you're drowning, they're the rock you can hold onto.

Love isn't about control. It's not holding on so tight, the other person feels suffocated or trapped. Love gives the other permission to do their own thing, figure things out, have separate friends, enjoy different hobbies, be alone and not feel threatened. There's trust in the relationship and with trust, there's never a need to control.

Love is built on a solid foundation of friendship. Lust and passion might be there, but the friendship is what holds the two of you together. When the physical intimacy ebbs and flows (and sometimes becomes dormant for a while), the friendship is the connective tissue that holds you together.

Love isn't just a feeling. It's a choice. It's a decision you make every day, to stick with that person. It's not always an easy choice.

It's also not always the right choice for some people. We all know couples who shouldn't be together or have friends in abusive or loveless marriages that we hope choose to get the hell outta there. Or like me, have truly tried everything to make it work and eventually have to accept they are better off apart. For those people, the most loving choice they can make is to choose themselves. Love themselves enough to give themselves permission to leave when it no longer feels like love.

Chris reminds me of what love should feel like. When I saw him recently, just being in his presence reminded me that love doesn't care about time or distance or what the other looks like or what either of you have been through. It doesn't care about how much money you make or your accomplishments or what title you hold at a job or whether you work at all. It doesn't care about impressing the other person or working hard to be liked.

It's the feeling that this person gets you and always will. You'll both change and grow, and your love will change and grow with it. It's knowing the person you're with wants your happiness as much as they want it for themselves. It feels non judgy. It doesn't compare you to someone else and wishes you were different. It doesn't project all of their unresolved stuff onto you. No, love is content in the simple act of *being together.*

And although Chris and I are only friends all these years later, I owe him a debt of gratitude for reminding me what love is *supposed* to feel like, so I recognize it when it comes around again. And maybe it's a good reminder to you as well.

Dina Strada

Chapter 12
When People Walk Away

If I'm honest, I used to see people who left my life as a rejection of me and proof of my not enoughness. Now I see these encounters as great teachers and thank them for the lessons.

I am often asked by people—who were in the beginning phases of a relationship or already deeply committed to another person—why the other person walked away and gave up on the relationship.

There are no easy answers, nor are they ever the same. We all choose to walk away from things for a variety of reasons, which are personal to us. But I'm a big believer in soul connections and that nothing is a coincidence in life, so I believe that each of those relationships was meant to be *something* for both people involved.

One of my favorite spiritual teachers calls the walking away from a relationship a "forfeiture." It's when two people are brought together with the intention and hope that they will take the opportunity to create something together but then one person withdraws prematurely.

It was not an accident or blind chance that we've met. That person was brought to us because we were asking for what they had to offer in some way, whether it was through prayers, the energy we were sending out or even through our thoughts, which we may have never verbalized to anyone.

But sometimes we don't recognize what it is or what it's meant to be right away, and we give up on it too soon. Maybe it looked different than we thought it should. Maybe it was taking too long to get off the ground, and we lost interest and patience. Maybe we were going to have to put work into it to create what we wanted, and in today's world most of us don't have the time or energy to work hard at anything, especially a relationship. We want it to be easy. Well, at least I want that!

So, in turn, without even realizing it, we "forfeit" the opportunity given to us to create something we really wanted or to learn a lesson our soul needed. And that's our choice. We can move on and tell ourselves, "It just wasn't meant to be." We forfeit the opportunity for growth and expansion.

But for the person who didn't forfeit and throw in the towel prematurely, it can be heartbreaking and difficult to not personalize it and make it about us. Although it's hard to not feel rejected, it's important that we understand it truly isn't about us but about the other person's readiness and willingness to meet us where we are.

Here's what we need to understand about relationships and love:

We are given opportunities to connect in deeply intimate ways with people as we move through life. Most of these people are brought into our spheres because they have something beautiful and valuable to offer us. But we don't have to accept them at that moment in time if we're not ready. We should listen to ourselves. Trust our gut. Discern whether the opportunity is one we want to take because we don't have to if it doesn't feel right.

People walk away from love and relationships for many reasons. Sometimes it's out of fear; fear of being vulnerable or getting hurt. Fear of losing our independence or thinking we have to give up our current lifestyle and freedom. Fear of our feelings not being reciprocated or that we somehow won't be able to measure up and give the other person what they want. Most often it's fear of something from our past repeating itself and that the relationship might turn out like a past one that was painful.

Sometimes people walk away because love or having a relationship isn't a priority in their lives and they have other things they feel they need to do first. Most of us who have been in love know that love forces us to make compromises, go into uncomfortable places, and look at things within ourselves that we don't want to see. These things can be enough to make us want to walk away when there are things we still want to do or deep places we aren't willing to go.

Intimate relationships bring out our shadow sides. Another person's love often shines a light on those places within ourselves that we've kept hidden and don't want to face. Another person's desire to connect with us so intimately can start to feel painfully uncomfortable, and we may not be ready to delve into that shadow stuff and work on it.

And sometimes people walk away because they aren't able to recognize the opportunity for growth and expansion being given to them or a good thing when they see it! It's okay. We all do things when we're ready. Besides, the universe, God, fate, or whatever you believe in will find another way, often through another person to give us a second chance at having what we want or what our soul needs to grow.

I've learned a lot about what I want and who I am through every relationship, no matter how brief or casual they were, including the ones I myself forfeited and walked away from.

I've learned that it's better to have nobody than somebody who is half in or not in it at all.

I've learned that I'm not willing to be in a relationship that forces me to prove my worth or pretend to be someone I'm not.

I've come to understand that just because another person wants something more from me, if I'm not in a place where it aligns with

what I want and where I'm at, I can forfeit the opportunity without guilt or feeling like I'm letting the other person down.
I've learned that being vulnerable and open is always worth it, even when the other person doesn't give the same back to me. Because by doing this we are honoring ourselves by *being* ourselves and at the end of the day *that's* the person we want someone to love.

So, as you move through the pain of a broken heart or grieve the loss of something that had just started and didn't go where you'd hoped it would, grieve it without personalizing it. Continue to put yourself out there, trusting that the next time maybe nobody will forfeit the opportunity before the gift of the two of you coming together is revealed.

Chapter 13
Is It Over?
5 Signs It's Time to Let Them Go

If I'm honest, one of the most courageous decisions I've ever made is letting go of something that was constantly hurting my heart and soul, no matter how much I wanted to hold on for dear life.

I've walked away from things both big and small in my life.

The big things included a marriage that for many reasons was no longer meant to be as awful and painful as that was.

The smaller things were relationships and friendships that took up way too much energy or felt one-sided.

Years ago, I decided to walk away from an amazing job I'd been at for over 20 years—with no plan, no other job lined up, and two young children to support.

The movie studio I worked for at the time had been acquired by another large company and I was one of the few people who didn't lose my job in the merger. Yet, I found myself voluntarily walking away from the job at a time the market was flooded with unemployed people. Some people probably thought I was crazy, and maybe even a bit irresponsible for taking that risk.

But other people told me I was brave.

Looking back, although the months following leaving that job were difficult and scary, I knew what I had done was the right thing for me and divine timing. I had reached a point in my life where honoring my heart and being true to what my soul was longing for was far more important than living in fear of "what if" and complacency.

I have been raised with the "suck it up" and persevere even when things are hard mentality. Life has its challenges for all of us and my parents taught us to not give up and walk away from things, but to instead push through and stick with it even when things got hard. None of the Strada kids are quitters, and it's been our perseverance throughout our lives that has led all 3 of us, including my brother and sister, to being successful.

But I admit I had been doing what so many of us do. We stay in relationships, marriages, jobs, business partnerships, financial investments, and even friendships because we convince ourselves it's not that bad and things will get better. Maybe we tell ourselves we have no other options or that we won't survive financially if we leave. We scare ourselves into thinking we can't leave the crappy, loveless marriage and raise our children alone. Or walk away from a soul sucking job because "it pays the bills".

And often we can't seem to escape the fear that haunts us most, "What if I don't find something better?"

We can't attract something better until we let go of what's no longer serving us to make room for something else to come in. The choice to walk away may seem daunting or have consequences we're not ready to yet face, but we don't have to stay in something that's making us miserable, disempowering us, or hurting our hearts. I can't tell you how many people I know got their big break, met the love of their life, or called in something beyond their wildest imagination when they finally let go of the thing that was weighing them down.

After I left that job, which was honestly a dream job (everyone who worked for DreamWorks Animation can vouch for how lucky we were to work there), I'm still asked, "Why did you walk away? How did you know it was time?" It hasn't been just that job I've walked away from.

I've walked away from plenty of relationships, even one or two friendships that were incredibly hard to let go of. I walked away from living in LA which was my home for over 20 years, to move back to NJ where I grew up.

When we decide to walk away from something or someone is different for everyone. We all have varying levels of tolerance, circumstances that force us to stay in things longer than we want, or reasons we hold onto things. But these, for me, are some clear, tell-tale signs that it's time to let something or someone go:

1. Our bodies keep the score.
Our bodies are the number one indicator that something isn't right and our internal warning system that things need to change. Low levels of energy, anxiety, chronic fatigue, migraines, insomnia, stomach issues, panic attacks, depression or constantly getting sick are the most common signs and biggest indicators that we need to make changes in our life. Listen to your body! Every physical symptom we have is a manifestation of our spiritual and emotional state.

2. Unexplained mood swings.
Your once optimistic and cheery personality has turned to anger, bitterness, and pessimism. Little things set you off. You have no patience. You start overreacting to things you used to be able to let go. You cry at the drop of a hat. This doesn't mean that you're crazy, overreacting, or unjustified in feeling what you feel—especially if you're in a relationship, marriage, job, or situation that constantly makes you feel this way. It means the person has probably crossed your boundaries far too many times, not shown up for you or doesn't listen when you've told them over and over what you need. Or the situation is making you so miserable, you can no longer push through and make it work. When we start becoming someone we're not (often someone we don't like), it's typically a sign we've had enough and it's time to move on.

3. We feel disrespected and unappreciated.
For every person in our life who doesn't value or appreciate what we bring to the table—trust me, there are at least 10 other people in their place who will. The problem is we get comfortable or used to being treated a certain way and start to believe there's nothing better out there. Or we may be financially entangled or have kids together so feel we can't leave. Feeling disrespected, unseen, and undervalued may start to feel normal, and this should *never* feel normal for any of us.

Obviously the first thing we need to do when we're feeling this way is have a conversation with the other person to communicate how we're feeling and give them an opportunity to try to fix things and make them better. Sometimes though people can't accept what we're telling them, or they don't agree, so they don't know how to change their behavior. If we've had the same conversation with them multiple times, and things *still* don't change and they continue to behave in the same way we've told them doesn't work for us, then there's nothing left to be said, and you have to decide whether it's worth it to stay and continue to be treated that way.

4. The universe starts giving us signs.
Many years ago, I took a freelance job on top of my full-time job. I knew it was too much, but I had already committed to the project and wanted to honor my word and complete it. I just didn't know how to say no and back out.

In comes the Universe to fix the situation! First, I got bronchitis and was laid out for a week. Then, my laptop crashed and I was forced to take a break from the freelance project for two weeks until it got fixed. Next, I got tendinitis in my right hand, and the doctor told me I couldn't type or use the computer for 4 weeks. I couldn't deny that I was clearly getting a bunch of signs telling me to *stop and let it go*. I wasn't thrilled with this message, but I finally relented and let the freelance job go. Best decision ever!

5. Other opportunities start showing up more aligned with us.
I've had friends tell me that when they seriously considered leaving a
relationship, they noticed other people flirting or expressing interest
in them. Or, when they gave serious thought to leaving a job, they
were approached by a headhunter or a friend at another company
they were really interested in about a great opportunity they weren't
even looking for.

These are clear signs that it's time to let go of whatever you're
holding onto. The signs are a way of telling us we're safe, that if we
take the chance, we'll be supported because there's *something better
out there.*

Heed the signs. Intuitively, we all know when it's time to walk away
from something. **Don't let fear stop you. Don't let the "what ifs" stop
you. Don't let what's happened in the past stop you. Just *do it.* Don't
look back in the rearview mirror and don't project and worry about
the future.** You've got no business there.

If what you're holding onto is meant to come back around at a later
date, it will. Trust that! But listen to your body, your heart, and the
other signposts and synchronicities showing up in your life. They are
all trying to tell you something.

The first step toward anything great in my life came when I was
willing to be fearless in the face of being scared and unsure. I've
learned to surrender and trust myself. Because at the end of the day,
the only person we can *always* trust to tell us the truth is ourselves.

Dina Strada

Chapter 14
Don't Give Yourself Away Too Quickly

If I'm honest, one of the biggest mistakes I've made in my relationships is having expectations of someone I barely knew.

It's amazing how quickly we put our expectations on people after just meeting them.

It's natural to get excited and hopeful when we meet someone we totally vibe with. It's true that maybe the market of available people has widened and become more accessible due to online dating apps, but finding someone we actually click with is something special.

I acknowledge over the years I've become a bit pickier and maybe even overly cautious. Maybe it's because I've been hurt or disappointed so many times that every flag I see I make into a big fat red one without giving people a fair shot. So, if I actually connect with someone on a deep level, I can sometimes jump the gun and give my heart away far too quickly. I had to learn the hard way that my natural inclination toward being trusting and giving with my heart before I really got to know what someone's intentions were is a recipe for disaster. One that usually ends with me swearing off dating for another 10 years.

Of course, we want to believe someone's intentions are in alignment with ours when we first start out. But the truth is, we're complicated creatures. Even when we say we know what we want, we often don't. And in this swipe right on Friday night, swipe right again Saturday night culture where endless options are available to us, exercising a little caution before getting too excited about someone needs to become the norm.

PRACTICING DISCERNMENT IN RELATIONSHIPS

After a particularly heartbreaking relationship a few years ago (one where I consciously worked hard to not get emotionally invested but failed) I chose to take a hiatus from dating or having sex. Friends scoffed in horror that I would deprive myself so long from carnal pleasures. "You haven't had sex in over a *year*? Why would you do that to yourself?" one friend asked.

"I've never been happier," I responded gleefully. "No drama in my life!"

It was true. There were no unproductive days at work because I was constantly checking my phone for someone's text message. No hour-long conversations with friends dissecting the behavior of some guy who failed to call me in the expected lot of time after I had gone out with him. No more keeping my free nights open until the last minute on the off chance said guy would want to see me. It was honestly the most peace I'd felt in a long time. I was doing me, and that felt great.

I think sometimes we can give our hearts away prematurely. In our quest to find that perfect love or fulfill some unrealistic fantasy we have in our heads of what the ideal relationship is, we can jump into things too quickly without giving the relationship time to breathe and organically find its own way. I've seen many men and women not taking the time to really get to know someone and ignoring the obvious things that won't work in the relationship simply because they want it to work so badly.

Then we find ourselves falling in love with the *idea* of someone or projecting our relationship fantasies onto them instead of seeing who they actually are. We tolerate behaviors that don't work for us because we're too scared to be alone.

But you know what? Being alone is a whole lot better than being with someone who can't meet us where we are. It hurts a whole lot less to be honest about that up front and know what we want than to settle for something we don't.

I love myself far more than I love the idea of being with another person. I have become a master at discernment. If I go out on a date with someone, it's because I've taken the time to get to know them as a friend first. I'm honest about what I'm looking for and what I'm not. I make sure I allow ample time to get a sense of their character, how they treat other people in their life from the waiter to their mother and their willingness to show up for me before I get emotionally attached or become invested in the relationship.

Discernment is so important. It's about trusting your gut. It's having the ability to judge wisely using your intuition about whether someone is worthy of your time and energy.

Sure, you can be vulnerable. But be vulnerable while practicing discernment. Ask yourself first, "Do I really know this person well enough to invest my heart? Can I have an honest conversation with them without fear that they'll run away? Have they told me what they're looking for and is it what I *actually want?*"

If the answer is no, don't give your heart away. Don't settle. Give it more time. Reign in your expectations and wait until you're on the same page. And if you find after giving it the appropriate amount of time that you're not, don't be scared to walk away and open yourself up to finding someone who is.

Your heart is precious and sacred. Treat it that way and for God's sake, don't accept anything less than what you truly want. I promise you, something else will come around if you have the courage to let go of something or someone that just doesn't make you feel good.

Dina Strada

Chapter 15
The Biggest Mistakes We Make in Our Relationships

If I'm honest, the biggest mistake I've made in relationships is letting someone stay in my life far longer than they deserved to. When I let those people go, it created space for something better to come in.

When I think back to every relationship I've been in, I'm always a bit nostalgic reliving the early stages of the courtship.

Those butterflies in the stomach before seeing each other, the flirty text messages, and the wild chemistry that simmered beneath the surface every time we were in a room together.

And the sex. Oh, good God, the sex.

There's nothing that can compare to those first few months of exploring each other's bodies–the relentless need to stay awake till all hours of the night engaging in multiple rounds of delicious foreplay followed by exquisite lovemaking, and the insatiable desire to forego hunger, thirst, and sleep just for the sheer delight of pleasuring each other.

Which is why it's no surprise that many of us overlook the very things we know ended the person's last relationship, and that are screaming at us relentlessly in the background behind this blissful, pink cloud like a smoke alarm trying to warn us of an impending fire.

We all know what this looks like. It's the guy we jump into a relationship with, knowing he has a history of being emotionally unavailable.

It's the smoking hot woman we've lusted after for months who finally gives us a shot when we know she's been indecisive and dismissive with men, typically dropping them like a hot potato when the next best thing comes along.

It's the person we know has cheated on their last few partners yet has managed to convince us that they were unfaithful because their needs weren't being met in their prior relationship, or their ex was a total prick, or they simply "weren't happy" and for whatever reason acted out.

So, we make the biggest mistake that's very easy to make in any new relationship…We believe *we'll* be different. We believe *they'll* be different. Because they're *with us* now.

If you're reading this and you felt that little punch in the gut accompanied by a slight wave of nausea because it sounds like I may be talking about you—read on. I'm most certainly talking about you (and me at one time in my life).

I used to be on an endless quest to prove to myself that I was special. I needed validation that I was different from every other girl a man had ever been with. I needed to prove that I was so damn lovable, whatever patterns some guy had coming into the relationship with me—whether it be a history of infidelity, neediness, the inability to commit, lover of the chase but never the prize syndrome, or emotionally unavailable—I convinced myself that I was the cure for it.

As it turned out *I am not the cure for any of these things*, nor are you and I can assure you that every relationship I had with someone who exhibited these patterns ended with, I'll let you guess…
Disappointment and heartbreak with yours truly in the starring role! GOD, I hated that part.

So, here's where we have to start being radically honest with ourselves. When we start any new relationship, it's important to go in with our eyes wide open and the willingness to put our romantic fantasies aside for a moment and to get real with ourselves.

We have to first be willing to ask some of the unromantic questions of our partner to get as much information as we can about who that person really is underneath all that smoldering sexiness and charisma and learn more about what their past relationships have been like and how they felt being in them. I'm not a fan of "interviewing" someone on a date. Nobody wants to be interrogated.

But we do need to have deeper conversations other than, "your place or mine"?

Some of my friends have admitted that they wouldn't share the uglier parts of their past with someone because they want to present their best selves to the person they're interested in. It's normal for most of us to give our own version of what went wrong in our past relationships and omit any details that paint us in a poor light.

But I'd much prefer somebody be completely transparent with me and share what they think went wrong in previous relationships and what they've learned about themselves from them because it shows me a level of self-awareness I'm looking for in another person.

More often than not, I believe that most people are willing to be at least partly honest about their pasts. They may not divulge all the dirty details and that's totally legit. Who wants to dwell on the past, especially if we've done things we haven't exactly been proud of? We're entitled to keep parts of our lives private if that's what we so choose.

But I do think we have to be willing to ask more questions as we're getting to know someone in a new relationship. As we get to know someone on a deeper level and move past the honeymoon phase, that's where we discover things about a person that we get to decide will or won't work for us. I dated someone years ago who was a hottie and a total catch but never sustained a relationship longer than 3-4 months with anyone. That told me something about him right from the get-go. Either he wasn't emotionally available, or he couldn't get vulnerable enough to take things to the next level with someone or maybe he wasn't a long-term kind of guy. Either way, I didn't think I was going to be the one to change him. Instead, I looked at him as someone to enjoy time with (and enjoy I did) and if it lasted beyond 3 months, great. If it didn't, I wouldn't say I was surprised.

It lasted exactly 3 months.

And here's the thing; I'm not saying things can't work out with someone who maybe hasn't had a ton of luck in their past relationships. We might be the exact person that person has been looking for all along! Or maybe we're the person they need in their life right now to help heal some wound, create some kind of transformation, or be the catalyst to that person's growth and them to ours. That's often why two people are brought together in the first place even if it's not a forever thing.

What I *am* saying is that we can't act surprised or be indignant, angry, or disappointed if someone ends up doing the very same thing to us that they did in their last relationship. Patterns are really tough to break, even when we're doing conscious work on ourselves to break them.

For example, we can't claim to be shocked if someone who cheated on their last partner with us then cheats on us with someone else. I did this once and had the balls to say "Well, I never thought they would do that to *me!*"

I mean, really. So dumb. My father literally said to me one time, "I mean Dina, are you really that stupid?"

So, ladies and guys... eyes wide open. Have realistic expectations. Talk about the hard stuff.

Be brutally honest about your wants, desires, and questions right up front.

Don't get all caught up in the butterflies, and chemistry, and all-night sex-a-thons without having those heartfelt conversations with yourself and the other person about where you're both at before jumping into the deep end together.

STILL, THERE ARE OTHER MISTAKES WE MAKE IN OUR RELATIONSHIPS

There are small things we do that hurt our relationships and then there are the BIGGIES. The BIGGIES are the ones that make our relationships fall apart. If you've got someone in your life who you currently feel like things are going south between the two of you, I can guarantee you're doing one or all these things:

1. You're not communicating.
This is the #1 worst offender that kills relationships. We don't communicate what we want or need, when we're upset, hurt, or when the other person does something we don't understand. We just stay silent. In working with clients, I can't recount all the times when they're upset about a situation and I ask, "Have you said something to this person about how you feel?" their response is a defensive "Well no...I'm not saying anything!"

Okay, great. Then expect that relationship will *never* be what you want. People can't give us what we want or need if we don't tell them what's wrong in the first place. Honest communication is the crux of every great relationship. Having difficult conversations suck but can bring you to a deeper, more intimate level with someone you care about. Giving someone the benefit of the doubt and being willing to go to those hard places with them and say what's in your heart—that's what leads to expansive relationships. Not staying silent.

2. You make assumptions.

I had a boss tell me recently the greatest piece of advice she ever got from one of her bosses was to *never assume*. I loved it! No more saying, "Oh, well I assumed they were following up on that" at work anymore. Or "I assumed you knew what I meant." Nope. THEY DIDN'T. YOU JUST ASSUMED!

Assumptions are the root of all evil. You assume your co-worker is going to take the initiative and send an email out to everyone you just had a meeting with recapping action items. You assume your boss knows you want to be promoted because they see how hard you've been working. You assume your friend is too busy for you or blowing you off because they haven't reached out for a while. I was once really upset with a friend who wasn't getting back to me or reaching out, only to find out she had just found out her mother was dying and was barely getting through her days. Again, if you want your relationships to thrive and be authentic, don't make assumptions, then go back and read #1.

3. You keep "score."

If you often hear yourself saying, "I feel like I put way more into this relationship than they do," it may be time to do some inner reflection and bring it back to yourself. Relationships aren't transactional. We should give because we want to give and do because we want to do. If you're running a tally of how much you do versus how much they do, the other person will always come up short.

Those are transactional relationships. In friendships, there will be times when a friend may need more from us if they're going through a difficult time. We may find we're giving way more than we're receiving at that moment. But none of us are immune to being needy at times and hopefully when we go through a difficult time ourselves, those same people will be there for us.

Things aren't always in perfect balance in relationships. The key is discerning temporary and situational imbalance from a long-standing issue that never changes. We always have the choice to give more or less in all of our relationships. We also have the choice and responsibility to *communicate how we're feeling.* A genuine, authentic relationship of any kind is not based on keeping score. If you're a score keeper, you'll always be the loser.

4. You're waiting around for them to change.

I once had a client say to me about a guy she was dating, "He's such a great guy, but really needs to work on himself. I think if I give him more time, he'll get there and then I think we could have a great relationship."

Waiting for a person to change, become who you want them to be or grow into their potential is not a great choice for either of you. We can choose to accept and love people unconditionally for who they are and where they're at, or we can expend a whole lot of energy wanting, praying, and waiting for them to be different. If someone you cared about was waiting for *you* to be different, how would you feel? We all want to be accepted for who we are. Waiting for somebody to be someone they're not doesn't just dishonor you, but them as well.

5. You're not fully present.

I'm so guilty of this one. I see it all the time; couples out to dinner, co-workers in a meeting, families at the dinner table and nobody is talking to each other or making eye contact. Instead, they're looking down at their phones. I'm guilty of this with my own kids, being physically there, but not really being present. I may be on the couch watching a movie with them, but the entire time, I'm on my laptop or responding to texts on my phone.

People know when we're not present. They feel it. They see it in our body language. They sense it. And it breeds feelings of resentment and makes them feel unimportant. The greatest gift we can give to anyone we care about is our full attention when we're together.

6. You expect too little.
Sometimes we expect *too* much from people then are disappointed when they don't deliver. Then there's the rose-colored glasses phenomenon. We're so excited about landing that new job we've always wanted that we tolerate any kind of treatment. I had a friend who was so excited to be working with one of his mentors that he accepted insanely low pay, worked 80-hour weeks, and was told by his boss that "vacations are for the weak." He was so stressed he ended up in the hospital.

In our closest relationships, we can often overlook some really bad or even indifferent behavior. The person doesn't respond when you reach out to them. They don't make you a priority. They talk down to you or are constantly disrespectful. Sometimes we need another person close to us to bring it to our attention to really see it. But when we do finally see it, hell girl - communicate that that shit is unacceptable and if it doesn't change get the hell outta there! You *know* you're worth more.

7. You stay far too long in the relationship.
We've all done this, especially with jobs. Hard to break up with those benefits! We know it's not working. We might be in a toxic or unhealthy relationship. Or in a friendship that's run its course. We're done and we know it. In fact, everybody knows it because we can't stop bitching about it. By the time we decide to walk away, irreparable bitterness, anger, and sometimes even betrayal have festered. Cheating and affairs are often by products of staying in relationships far too long that haven't been working for a long time.

I have two close friends who shared a tumultuous relationship but stayed in it for the sake of the friendship group we were all in together. They were always fighting and neither felt respected by the other person. Conversely, neither of them wanted to be the bad guy and sever ties because they didn't want to break up our group. They remained in the friendship, which wasn't really an authentic friendship, for far too long. Finally, their pent-up resentment, anger and bitterness exploded on a trip together and things were said in the heat of anger that couldn't be taken back. After that they finally parted ways, but it was an ugly ending.

When a relationship has run its course, we can part on better terms without all the anger and bitterness just by being real about it and having a totally honest conversation that things aren't working out and it might be time to part ways. Think about how many times you've stayed in a job far longer than you knew you should then ended up getting fired (the universe's way of rescuing you) or had a full-blown meltdown that finally convinced you to leave. I have friends who've needed to get to the point of having nervous breakdowns, getting really sick, or being put out by their doctors on medical leave to convince them it was time to go. Why go through all of that when your heart told you it was time to leave long before it got to that point?

Our hearts know when it's time. Listen to your inner voice. All relationships are not meant to last forever regardless of whether they're professional, partnerships, friendships, and for some people even family. When you're trying to make the decision whether to stay or go, I find sitting silently and feeling into my body helps me answer the question. Our bodies don't lie. Deep down we really do know the right thing to do.

Dina Strada

Chapter 16
On Friendship

If I'm honest, my friendships have been the glue that have held me together through the messiest, ugliest parts of my life and the mirrors that have reflected back the most beautiful parts of myself.

Let's admit that friendships are both complicated and amazing.

Complicated because our expectations of friends can be ridiculously high and amazing because they are some of the deepest, most profound, and unconditionally loving relationships we'll ever have in our life.

If you want great friends, then you have one simplest task... you've got to *be* a great friend. You need to treat your friendships like any other relationship in your life, one that ebbs and flows and changes as you change, grow older, and transition through different phases of life. And for God's sake, let go of the idea that you'll never fight or get on each other's nerves! Because friends who love each other deeply are human beings and make mistakes. Great friends, lifelong friends, ride or die friends...those are the ones who see you at your worst and love you anyway.

I see people grieve friendships that have ended or changed over the years. I get it. I too have some close friends who I grew apart from for reasons neither of us understood at the time. I've had friendships that were for a season of my life and then disappeared as unexpectedly as they came in and others where we had a falling out we simply couldn't repair. I've examined each of those relationships in my life with the intention of looking at my part and what I could have done differently.

I'll admit, the perfectionist, good girl part of me wants to blame myself for those friendships changing over time. *Why wasn't I enough? Why don't they want to be my friend anymore? What did I do wrong? Am I not lovable? I must have said something horrible and insensitive that pissed them off. I'm a bad person. It's all my fault!*

And you know what? Sometimes, it *is* our fault. Sometimes we don't show up as our best selves. Sometimes we think because we're friends we can say anything we want to that person with no tact or regard for their feelings. We can take the people we love most for granted, believing they will always be there. I like to think of relationships, especially friendships like plants. If we fail to water it, tend to it, check on it and give it some love we can't expect it to bloom or grow. Friendships require nurturing. Without it, they wither and die.

Our friendships require grace and understanding and sometimes a little space.

They require honest and loving communication, especially when we get triggered or hurt.

They require forgiveness, a lack of judgment when we so adamantly want to judge, compassion, empathy, and patience.

But most importantly, they require acceptance of the other person for exactly who they are and exactly who they aren't. Because without that, you'll be sitting on your judgment High Horse constantly. And let me be frank, nobody wants a judgmental friend so ya all need to check yourself and find different friends because authentic friendships that bi-pass the superficial require unconditional love for who we are.

I have been blessed in this lifetime with more close friendships than I sometimes feel I deserve. Some people hit the lottery when it comes to looks, others are born into wealthy families, some with athletic, artistic, or musical talent.

Me.... I hit the friendship Mega Millions.

I have friends I met in Kindergarten and friends I didn't meet until I became a mom. My friends are scattered across the globe, but no matter where we live, how often we see each other or how much time passes, those friendships are as deep and rich as ever.

My closest friendships have a few things in common that make us solid. Yours may be held together by other things but what I believe makes true friendships stick are these things:

Honesty - We don't keep things from each other. We don't hide parts of ourselves. We don't tell each other what we want to hear but what we need to hear. Girl, if the pants make your ass look big, we're gonna tell ya! (We may not say it that way, but we'll tell you they aren't flattering). If the guy you're interested in is running full speed towards you waving 6 red flags, we're pointing that shit out. We're not here to make you feel good all of the time. We're here to protect you because we love you.

Non-judgment zone - We're all different and may tease each other for those differences but we don't judge them. I'm not a big drinker but my friends will stampede over you to get to their wine. I'm a determined, super organized Virgo and run myself up my own ass most of the time so I sometimes don't get my friends who live a more laid-back lifestyle, but I don't judge them. I know I have something to learn from those friends who actually know how to relax and have a good time! Thank GOD for them.

No score-keeping - Nobody likes a scorekeeper. Sometimes you'll be supporting me through some heavy shit, and I'll suck the life out of you with my extra-neediness and one day you'll need me to be that person for you. Maybe I'm always the one reaching out to make the plans but you're always the one calling me just to chat. It doesn't really matter because we each bring something of value to the friendship. If you're keeping score, you'll always feel you're getting the short end of the stick and that's not a friendship that will last for long.

Trust - My closest friends are the secret keepers. If I confide in them, they don't go blabbing my business all over town. The ones that have are people I keep at arm's length because I know I can't trust them. Trust is everything. Trust means you keep your word. Trust means you have integrity. Trust means honoring someone and holding space for them with anything they bring to you. Without it, you've got no foundation to build anything on.

Acceptance - If you're friends with me, you don't need to love everything about me. Like I've said, I'm a Type A, need to accomplish shit, neat freak Virgo who doesn't like to get too drunk or stay up late. *Boring!* But I'm also loyal as hell, nurturing, devoted to our friendship and can help you organize that dump truck of a closet of yours like nobody's business. We don't need to do things the same way, think alike or have the same taste but if we love each other, we accept each other exactly as we are, and exactly as we aren't.

How to Break Up with a Friend

My one friend shared how she was tired of, in some friendships, always being the one who had to reach out to make plans and stay connected, and that she didn't get much from those people's friendships anymore.

Another friend asked me if I thought it was okay to end a friendship with someone who'd made a snide comment about her to a mutual friend and had also been acting rude and standoffish with her recently.

I know people who literally can't stand someone in their friend group because they're an energy vampire and constantly negative, yet they'll stay in the friendship because they're too afraid to have the difficult conversation that needs to be had.

The Breakup Talk
Yes, we have the right to end friendships with people when they are no longer adding value to our lives.

Whether a friendship has become one-sided, the person has become an energy-sucking vampire or the two of you have just grown apart because your lives have drifted in different directions, when a relationship is no longer serving our highest good, it's perfectly okay and even healthy and empowering to end it.

But there is a right way and a wrong way to do this.

The wrong way is what I see happen most often. People ghost their friends. They just disappear and stop talking to us. One day, we may have gone out to dinner together and had what we thought was a great time, and the next minute that person is no longer returning our calls or texts. There's no explanation whatsoever, they've just dismissed us as if we were never friends at all.

This is never okay.

We owe every human being the decency of letting them know why we don't want to continue the friendship anymore, no matter how uncomfortable or difficult that conversation is gonna be. When we deny another person this, we don't give them an opportunity to understand what they've done to hurt us, or what they haven't done or what behavior they've exhibited during the friendship that's gotten us to this point. We also aren't giving the other person an opportunity to be heard themselves or clear up something that perhaps wasn't intentional or may have been a miscommunication.

Most importantly, and this I do feel we owe people, when we don't properly break up with a friend like we would in any other relationship, we deny that person the opportunity to learn and grow by sharing what they've done to push us away. You'd be surprised how many people are completely unaware that something they've said or done has alienated us or caused us to want to sever ties with them.

And sometimes, it's *us* who are behaving in ways that need to be called out, so that we don't continue the pattern of doing those things to other people.

Unless we communicate to that person what they've done and how they've hurt us, they won't know how to change their behavior in the future, so they don't lose other people in their life they care about.

This is the kindest and most honorable way to end a friendship:

1. Don't sever ties with a friend when angry.
All of us, at one time or another, have considered ending a friendship with someone when we're pissed as hell. But when our emotions are high and we're not thinking clearly, that is not the time to make major decisions about our relationship.

Cool down and give it some real thought before having the conversation. Talk about it with someone else you trust. An objective person will let you know if you're being unreasonable or if your decision to end your relationship is justified. Try not to do anything until you know you can have the conversation from a clear and level-headed place.

2. Choose the right time to talk.
Don't have this important conversation when you know there are limitations on the time you have together. Make sure you pick a time when you don't have anything scheduled right afterward, so if the conversation gets emotional or heated, you each have time and space

to center yourself and process what just happened. After all, you're about to drop a bomb on someone who isn't expecting it, so be considerate when you do it. Make sure they aren't on their way to work, to pick up their kids, or heading to an important social event. Ask them when a good time would be to have a serious conversation before scheduling it.

3. Be specific.
It's tempting to launch right into a blanket statement, "You always make me feel _______" or, "I'm sick and tired of you never being there for me."

The words *always* and *never* are rarely true. Instead, be specific. Give them examples of what they did specifically and how that made you *feel.* Maybe it's, "For the past several months, you've been dumping all your problems on me and never asking how *I'm* doing. It makes me feel like you don't care about *me*, and I've started to feel that the friendship is one-sided."

If we don't take the time to tell people specifically what behavior or actions have hurt us, they're left with having to guess or make assumptions, often incorrect ones. And we all know there's nothing worse than playing guessing games and spending a lifetime wondering what *really* happened.

4. Try to acknowledge the person for what their friendship meant to you.
This may be tough to do during a heated and ugly conversation, but if at all possible, take the time to acknowledge the person for what they got right. It can be as simple as, "I know this is really hard to take in, but I want you to know that I will always be grateful for the times you were there for me and the great memories we made together but... I need some distance right now." *And... buh-bye*

Many years ago, I had to break up with a friend and I'll admit in that moment I honestly couldn't stand the person. They sucked the life out of me every time we were together and had done some hurtful things. During that conversation the person was attacking me verbally and I just wanted to cut it off and be done. Still, I felt it was important to honor them for the time we shared together.   I was able to say as calmly as possible, "I'm sorry you're so upset right now and I'm grateful for the times you were a good friend to me but I think it's best we end the communication with each other now so we can both move forward." I don't know if the person felt any better hearing that, but I know I felt better saying it.

5. *Leave the door open.*
I've found the best way to end any friendship is to always leave the door open to the possibility that the two of you may decide to one day become friends again.

Sometimes what we really need is space and time apart. Whether we've grown apart, are at odds over a specific incident, or going through our own stuff and can't deal with the energy the friendship is taking up, we don't know how we're going to feel down the road. A great way to end the breakup conversation is with something like, *"Right now it's best for me to not have you in my life but maybe down the line I'll feel differently and want to reconnect. It's just not now."*

You'd be surprised how often you'll find yourself wanting to reach out to that very person months or even years down the road. You might go through something that makes you more compassionate and understanding about where that other person may have been in their own life when you ended the friendship. Sometimes, with time we have more perspective and are able to forgive someone for not being what we needed at the time.

So, if you feel it's necessary to break up with a friend, do what feels right. But give the person you're breaking up with the decency of closure.

We would have a conversation before breaking up with someone we're in a romantic relationship with (unless you're a ghoster), and our friends–who have sometimes been a part of our lives longer than any romance–deserve the same.

Dina Strada

Chapter 17
Mean Girls vs True Sisterhood

If I'm honest, I hate the word mean girl because it sounds super clique but girls, you gotta rein yourself in if you're guilty of any of what I'm about to divulge.

If you don't think you're a mean girl, I invite you to remain open while reading this chapter. Because let's admit, we've all had our mean girl moments. And I believe it's the mean girls who sometimes have no self-awareness that they're making other women feel awful about themselves. And really, we need to do better than this.

I watched a mean girl moment go down in front of my very eyes between grown women far too old for the kind of shit they pulled at a very big work event one time. It was subtle. There was no name calling or outright bullying. No obvious glaring looks at the other person that anyone else in the room would have noticed.

Instead, it was a deliberate act of exclusion. It was pushing the other person out of the way and being so condescending and dismissive that it made my blood boil.

Mean girls think that because they don't say directly "I don't like you, get outta my way bitch" to another woman's face that nobody notices their digs. Or that the other person on the receiving end of their mean girl behavior doesn't feel their obvious dislike or intention to push them aside, make them feel small, unimportant, or dismissed.

But we notice. Gurrrl... we see you.

We see women like this everywhere, and many of us have been their victims long after we suffered through it as teenagers or young girls.

My intention in talking about it is the hope that if you see even a little bit of yourself in what mean girl behavior looks like, you'll have a greater understanding of how it makes another woman feel and what it does to sisterhood as a whole.

Let's start with what sisterhood *doesn't* look like.

Sisterhood isn't about competing. It stems from the belief that there is plenty of abundance to go around so when we see one of our sisters accomplish something huge, like land the big job, move into her dream apartment or home, meet a fabulous partner, or get handed some unbelievable opportunity, we celebrate her. She's proof that we can have that too. We should feel inspired by her success and good fortune, knowing that when our time comes, they're going to be right there next to us celebrating with as much joy as we have celebrating them.

Sisterhood isn't about judging each other. Maybe another woman doesn't look her best or gained a little weight since the last time you saw her. Maybe she went back to that asshole everybody can see is gonna break her heart again. Maybe she's an exhausted mom feeding her kids Cheetos and sugary juice for breakfast because she's barely holding things together at home. It doesn't matter. Sisterhood is about compassion and empathy. We offer support and loving kindness, not judgment.

Sisterhood isn't thinking you're better than her. You're not prettier, smarter, hotter, richer, more accomplished, or more deserving of having something than she is. Remember there has probably been a time in your own life where you felt ugly, broke, had less experience, were unsure of yourself and lacked confidence. Sisterhood is knowing we're all equal and acknowledging we're all a work in progress. We're human just like her.

So, let me go back to the women I was working with. There was no evidence of sisterhood here. What I saw was competition, judgment and someone believing they were better than someone else. It made me sad because all of them were smart, bright, talented women who each had something of value to bring to the table and to each other. They had different experiences and backgrounds to contribute to the event and really could have learned from each other.

Instead, they chose to ice each other out, one of the women commenting, "I'm not even sure what she does," when that person had been working around the clock to help us deliver a phenomenal event.

I watched two of the women acting catty, whispering among themselves, and then going silent when the other woman walked up to them to ask a question. I observed the "looks" exchanged between them when she opened her mouth to offer up an idea. The curt dismissive, "I've got this" shot in her direction in front of a group of executives when she offered a suggestion on how to do something.

I felt, and maybe I was being overly sensitive, that they were annoyed with me for sitting next to the woman who was the target of their mean girl behavior as if I should have chosen sides and iced her out the way they did. I was never going to do that. We were a team, and I wanted that woman to know she was an important part of our team whether she was being treated that way by these other women or not.

My heart broke for her and at the same time I respected how brilliantly she handled herself, never once losing her cool, snapping back at them or being unprofessional. Instead, she smiled and said, "no problem" when they dismissed her input or ideas. She didn't take it personally (although how could you not) and went about her other responsibilities like a pro.

I see mean girl behavior in girls as young as 6 and 7 years old (I could share tales of pre-school drama my own daughter lived through) and in grown women old enough to qualify for a senior citizen discount.

When will we learn how to treat each other with respect, ladies? When will we finally learn to have each other's back?

I've listened to all the reasons over the years why someone believes they were completely in the right going at another woman or treating them like a piece of shit and I'm sorry, but I just don't buy it. Let's save the excuses please and grow up. It doesn't take a lot of effort to be kind to people and the world needs more of it. I myself can't justify my own mean girl behavior when I've acted out towards someone. I was wrong, period, end of story. I regret those moments in my life and have spent many years trying to understand *why* I behaved that way at that time and what was really going on beneath the surface to cause me to act like that.

I've come to realize that when we really don't like somebody, they have something to teach us. I think of those people as mirrors, reflecting back something we need to look at.

If someone is being short, condescending, or downright rude, I kill them with kindness. I keep the kindness up until they *have to give me a chance*. Even if they've already made up their mind that they don't like me for whatever reason, I refuse to give in and match their energy with the same negativity. I look hard for what they see in me they don't like and what I may not like in them and then ask the question, "what am I supposed to learn from this person?"

Most of the time we're being a mean girl because we just don't know the person. We've formed a preconceived judgment about them that's not even true based on what we see on the surface.

I ONCE ACTED LIKE A MEAN GIRL

Once upon a time, I hated another woman so much I would spit nails at her if I could. It was mean girl behavior at its finest. She was the woman my ex-husband loved and lived with after we split up, so I had my reasons (mostly jealousy), and she hated me equally as much.

The truth was, we simply *didn't know each other*. She hated me because he was married to me at one time, and I hated her because he now loved her.

I'd make snide comments about her to my friends and family even though she was gorgeous, successful, smart, and super cool. She made equally vicious comments about me to her friends and family even though maybe I'm not as gorgeous, but I *am* most definitely successful, smart, and super cool too!

My point is we decided we hated each other, and we didn't even know one another. We spent so much time being catty and judgmental towards each other without knowing each other personally. It was only 4 years later at a Starbucks on Ventura Blvd where we met up for the first time after the two of them broke up that we started the process of getting to know each other as women. And we were surprised to discover that we had more in common than we ever thought possible. I found myself not just liking her but really liking her as a person.

We shared similar insecurities and fears. We found comfort and strength in many of the same spiritual practices. We had a deep compassion for the experiences both of us had been through, and genuinely understood each other. When I finally put all my judgments aside about her because of my jealousy I clearly saw why my ex-husband had fallen in love with her. She was funny, sweet, smart, interesting, passionate about all the things my ex was into, that I didn't have much of an interest in. They had similar personalities and views on life. She was an all-around great woman even though she had done some not great things to me. And I realized that deciding we aren't going to like somebody is often rooted in jealousy or what someone did in a moment in time, instead of who they are as a person; the whole of them. And we have to look at the whole of a person.

I have some friends who have said to me, "You're a much bigger person than I am. I never would have made peace with someone who did what she did to you," But the thing is, you could. I believe we all can find compassion and forgiveness for someone if we believe they are just like us, human, and probably doing the best they know how at the moment.

You could if you believed that every woman is your sister. You could if you understood that every person deserves a 2nd chance and makes mistakes. Every woman is going through something, and we have more in common than we think. Even the ones who come in and rub you the wrong way, compete with you or hurt you. We heal by extending compassion, kindness and understanding towards each other, even when it's really friggin' hard.

Every one of us as women is dealing with something. EVERY ONE OF US. We all have insecurities, problems, struggles and fears. We're still fighting inequality, sexism, proving ourselves and a host of other issues men don't have to navigate.

Be a friend to a woman you see struggling. Mentor that young girl who is still rough around the edges and can't find her way in the workplace yet. Compliment someone you see on the street wearing an outfit you'd never be caught dead in because she's pulling it off (or maybe she's not but give the girl a high five that she has the confidence to wear it at all).

When someone is being a complete bitch, try offering them the benefit of the doubt. I watched a cashier at Trader Joes one time have zero reaction to a woman who was visibly impatient and losing her shit on her for taking too long to ring up her groceries. The cashier kindly handed the woman her change and said with not one ounce of sarcasm, "You seem to be having a tough day. I really hope it gets better." The bitchy woman was so taken off guard, she teared up and said, "I'm so sorry. My mother is in the hospital and I'm just sick to death with worry and trying to get to her before visiting hours are over."

Compassion. Understanding. Benefit of the doubt.

It's a beautiful thing when we can do it.

One time I snapped at a close friend who said nothing wrong because I was having a bad day and instead of snapping back at me, she said, "I love you and I know you've had a lot on your plate lately. I'm here if you need to talk." Do you know I remember that moment every single time someone snaps at *me*? (Thank you, Ariella). I now use that same line when someone else is having a rough day. That kindness and understanding... *God*, it goes a long way in co-creating sisterhood.

Ladies, please don't be the mean girl. Be the, "I'm here if you need to talk" girl. Be the, "Maybe I'm jealous of her" girl and get to know her better. Be the, "Maybe I just don't know her well enough" girl and take the time to get to know her.

Be the woman another woman remembers helped her when she needed it, celebrated her, rooted for her, forgave her, stood by her, mentored her, and made her feel good about herself. We have the choice to do that every single day for another woman.

All we have to do is decide which woman it is we want to be and then show up that way as often as we can. That's the way we create sisterhood.

Dina Strada

Chapter 18
Right Person, Wrong Time

If I'm honest, I see so many people who'd be great together that just met at the wrong time. I think accepting when this happens to us is one of the hardest things in the world and something we never forget.

Back in college, I was really moved by a Carl Jung quote I later used in an essay about love.

"The meeting of two personalities is like the contact of two chemical substances. If there is any reaction, both are transformed."

At the time, I had met someone who I would later end up with in one of the most beautiful relationships of my life.

Had you told me at the time we would end up together, I would have rolled my eyes and said it would never happen. We were two ships that kept passing in the night since meeting in my freshman year at Boston College. At first sight, there was an unexplainable spark and connection between the two of us.

We flirted relentlessly at work and at parties when we ran into each other. We hooked up a few times after getting drunk at a campus party and had relationships with other people but never with each other. We were friends who were fiercely attracted to each other and had great, great affection for one other.

By my junior year, as I was headed off for a semester abroad in London and we found ourselves saying our final goodbyes, we came to an appalling realization.

We were head over heels in love with each other.

Cue the record player scratching because this was shitty timing. I was dating someone else already and off to England in a matter of weeks. It was his senior year, so he was graduating before I returned to the states and had already made plans to move to London for work. We agreed with heavy hearts it wasn't meant to be and settled on keeping it a friendship.

My heart ached like never before. It felt wrong. *So wrong.* Like I had been given a beautiful perfect gift and I was told to never unwrap it.

The weeks leading up to my departure to England, I listened to the "mix tape" (yep, remember those from the 90s?) he had gifted me for Christmas and cried myself to sleep every night. I couldn't understand why we had never gotten the opportunity to be together when there was so much between us and how it was possible God was now going to whisk me so far away with this beautiful thing between us unfinished.

Two weeks before I was set to leave for England, there was a bombing on the tube in London and some other unrest in the country. It scared my parents enough to pull me from the program abroad and send me back to Boston instead of putting me on a plane to London.

The rest, as they say, is history. He and I got together soon after my triumphant return and had one of the best relationships of my life for over three years. People often ask me after I share this story whatever happened to him. We did talk about getting married after I graduated college, but I was still so young and didn't want to settle down so early in my life so eventually we went our separate ways. It was, however, one of the most transformative, amazing, and beautiful relationships of my life!

Lately, I have been surrounded by friends and clients coming undone, heartbroken over a person they have a deep soulful connection with that for one reason or another can't be explored. Physical distance, being in other relationships, fear, or timing have prevented them from being together and having a chance to explore what the connection is that exists between the two of them.

It can feel *soul crushing*, leaving us tossing and turning at night, unable to sleep or think about much else. When our heart recognizes another soul aligned with ours, it feels intense in our bodies. It manifests as an unrelenting *longing*, a pulsating desire that leaves us unable to think of anything else, and yet, no place to release. The soul is saying, "Yes! I recognize you. We've got some work to do together." And then under its breath mutters, "*But not now.*"

UGH. Horrible.

But don't fret! There's some good news here, at least what I've seen happen in my own experience. I have never encountered another person where we had that instant undeniable connection with each other who did not come back around eventually. *It's inevitable.* Like two magnets, you can't help but be drawn back together one day.

"There are only two mistakes one can make along the way to truth. One is not going all the way, and one is not starting." ~ Anonymous

Unexplainable connections with another person can be scary, especially if the person doesn't check all of our so-called "boxes." Maybe on paper they aren't what you say you're looking for, but trust me when I say, connections aren't about what you want; they've come along because of what you don't know you need.

That deep connection isn't always because the two of you are meant to be together in the traditional sense as a couple. Often these types of connections are to shake things up in your world, unravel things, or teach you something.

A perfect example of this... I have a friend who absolutely adores his wife. They've been together for over 20 years and are true soulmates and best friends. He met someone who he had a crazy, intense connection with at work. They were working on the same project together for close to 3 years so obviously spent a ton of time together. We'd get together for lunch, and he'd share with me how awful he felt because his connection with this woman was more than just attraction, it was a deep soul connection. There was absolutely nothing wrong in his marriage. No lack of sex. No lack of attention or time together. He had no desire to ever leave his wife and felt torn and conflicted about the time he was spending with this other woman who was also married.

Their connection eventually led to a brief emotional type of affair that both felt incredibly guilty over because they absolutely loved their spouses. There was never any crossing of physical boundaries, but their emotional intimacy was at times deeper than the one he shared with his wife.

Some people will scoff at this and immediately condemn them both for being unfaithful but as I listened to him share his internal struggle and feelings of guilt, I also saw something else I hadn't seen in him for many years... an aliveness! There was something this other woman opened up in him that I'd never seen. He had struggled over the years with some self-worth issues that he never had resolved in all the years he'd been single or married but through their time together, this woman healed something inside of him because she also struggled with the same thing. Inside of their relationship, they both healed.

He knew when their time together was ending because he felt the shift in himself and told me he understood why she had come into his life. He knew it was meant to be for a season, and the reason was to help him deal with these things that had been holding him back in many ways his whole life. He never wavered in his love and devotion to his wife, and they are still together today and happier than ever.

Right person maybe but wrong timing. Had they met 20 years earlier, maybe they *would* have ended up together for a lifetime but instead, they offered each other something they each needed at that moment, and then moved on with their individual lives.

What I can offer you is this...whatever the connection is that you have with another person, give it space and air to breathe. Release all attachment to it. You can't force what isn't meant for you right now. The universe works in divine timing, not yours.

Maybe the person has come into your life for another reason that hasn't yet revealed itself to you. They may have come in as a mirror to force you to look at something about yourself you haven't been willing to see. Or to make you question a relationship you're already in and ask yourself, "Is this really it? Am I really happy?"

Up until this point in my life, every single person I felt that unexplainable spark and connection with the moment we met came back around later. In some instances, it took *years* but was always worth the wait.

Timing is everything. Trust that what you're desiring will show up when you are most ready to receive it.

Chapter 19
Soulmates We'll Meet
and Love in this Lifetime

"If I'm honest, connections with soulmates can be both beautiful or heart-wrenching but without them, we wouldn't grow into everything we're meant to be on this earth."

The most Important encounters are planned by the souls long before the bodies meet each other." ~ Paulo Coelho

Most of us have met many different soulmates in our lifetime. All of them are deeply meaningful, intensely connective, and profoundly impactful on our lives.

Some soulmates stay around forever if we're lucky. Others leave more quickly than we want them to but leave a lasting impression on our hearts.

What I see people most struggle with is feeling a deep, soulful connection with another person who is not meant to be in their life forever and then having to go through the process of accepting that they need to let them go.

Not all soulmates are made of the feel good "we fell in love the moment our eyes met and are going to love each other till the end of time" kind. There are many other types of soulmates, ones who come in solely for the purpose of teaching us something, some to break apart our life to redirect us somewhere better and some who pass us for the briefest of moments yet tug on our hearts as if we've known them a lifetime.

These are just a few of the soulmates I've encountered in my own life, all of them captivating, memorable, and absolutely necessary for my soul's growth. Maybe you'll recognize them in your own.

1) *Friendship Soulmate*
Sometimes we meet a person and click from the moment we lay eyes on each other. It's as if we've known each other our entire life. You tell each other everything. You could talk for hours and never get tired being together. You share everything about yourselves with each other and never pass judgment. The two of you are always in sync as if you've known each other several lifetimes (and that's because you have!)

These types of soulmates may know you better than you know yourself, which is why they are extremely important in your life. They "get you" in ways nobody else does and have been brought into your life to help you navigate all of life's trials and triumphs, successes and failures and everything in between.

The friendship soulmate is a precious gift and one you should treasure because they are typically here to stay for a lifetime.

2) *The Wrecking Ball Soulmate*
This soulmate is not somebody that comes into our life peacefully. They enter to shake things up. They challenge us and make us question everything we thought we knew to be true about ourselves and our lives. There is a clear "before them" and "after them" distinction when we look back on our lives and realize that we are a completely different person because of their coming into our lives. This type of soulmate can come in many different forms but it's normally a romantic relationship that leaves us feeling as if we've been swept up like a tornado, taken for the ride of our life, and then dumped from the sky with no warning in an exhausted, tailspun heap. Affairs are often these types of soulmate connections, and they can be quite tumultuous, frenzied, and chaotic.

Despite feeling like we don't know what the hell happened since the ride was so fun when it first started, the beauty of this type of soulmate is that like a tornado hitting that leaves massive wreckage behind, we're forced to rebuild ourselves from the ground up when it's over. And when everything has been decimated, we have the opportunity to start anew and create something different. Maybe it's something that needed to change, needed to be destroyed so that something better could be rebuilt in its place.

The wrecking ball soulmate is hard and can be incredibly challenging. Souls that choose to come together in this way have taken on a really important job because they play such a huge part in our soul's growth. Although these relationships can be filled with longing, pain, and heartbreak most people leave the relationship and go on to rebuild something much more beautiful than what existed before.

3) *The Lover Soulmate*
These people don't stay in our lives forever. They come in as a lover and typically take on the form of a really beautiful relationship for a period of time. They might be our first love, an affair or simply a lover who we had a no-strings-attached unconventional relationship with.

These soulmates are meant to be in our lives for only a period of time to teach us about ourselves and other important lessons that will be poignant and meaningful down the road. Typically, these types of relationships don't start off with that "instant connection" feeling we associate with a long-term partner, but over time build and the relationship turns into something more serious and meaningful.

Soulmates like this often stay on good terms with each other after they part and remember their time together fondly. Years later, they will often look back at that person with gratitude for all they taught them and the special part they played in their life.

4) *Stranger Soulmates*
This is always a very brief encounter with a perfect stranger. It might be the person you sit next to on a flight for a few brief hours, someone you meet and spend time with one evening at a party, or as brief as a stranger whose eyes you meet on the street and exchange just a few words with.

Typically, the feeling is, "Oh! *I recognize you!*" Almost Deja vu, as if you've seen them before and are remembering them but can't place where. If you believe in past lives, it's typically because you are recognizing them as someone who truly is from your past.

The exchange is brief but intimate. They normally say something that you need to hear in that moment, validate something that you've been feeling or push you in a direction you need to go but are afraid. You know in the depths of your soul the encounter meant something even though you never see them again.

5) *Divine Love Soulmate:*
This is the soulmate that every one of us desires to have. And if we're lucky enough, we will meet them and live out the rest of our days on this earth together.

They encompass all of the above... the familiarity, the feeling of having known them for an entire lifetime moments after meeting them, the intense bond and connection that never goes away, the deep friendship, and the extraordinary, enchanted, deep-seated love.

May all of us have the good fortune of coming together with this person at some point in our lives. And if you've found this, how lucky you are to have been blessed with finding your forever soulmate!

Try not to put any expectations on a soulmate. Whether they come into your life for a moment, months, or years, treasure the deep connection you shared and know they were in your life for the exact time they were meant for. *That's what soulmates are all about. To* make their mark on your heart and leave when the lessons you were meant to learn through them are complete.

Section 3

Trusting the Journey

Chapter 20
You Gotta Feel It to Heal It

"If I'm honest, I spent much of my life resisting my true feelings. Anger made me feel wrong. Sadness made me feel weak. Needy made me feel "girly." Love made me feel scared. I became an expert at hiding when I was feeling anything remotely uncomfortable."

I grew up in a home where having feelings was considered healthy and even encouraged. Nobody said things to us like, "Stop your crying", "Suck it up" or "You shouldn't feel that way." Thank you, mom and dad, you were the best.

But it doesn't mean we grow up not feeling uncomfortable with certain feelings. For some men, vulnerability or crying can be difficult for them. Any feeling other than being in total control may feel scary.

For most women, anger is the #1 most uncomfortable emotion for us because we don't want to be perceived as bitchy (remember we grew up with boys poking fun at us when we got our periods and were feeling a little less perky than our normal selves!)

Some people numb their feelings with alcohol, drugs, shopping, smoking, or sex. I numbed with control. Being in control. Exerting control. Maintaining iron-will control over everything in my life, including my emotions.

The thing about the illusion of being in control is that it really only works for so long before the real emotions bubble to the surface, erupt like a dormant volcano and explode onto someone or something unintended. And trust me when I tell you, *that ain't pretty.*

I was fascinated watching the Netflix rage-fueled drama BEEF with Ali Wong and Steve Yeun, both brilliant actors. One of my favorite lines from Ali Wong's character Amy Lau is, "I *hate pretending that I don't hate things.*"

I mean, God, I could relate.

The show is based on a road rage incident between the two characters but really, underneath the road rage is what I'm referring to. It's the simmering of emotions that we've held onto for so long, that when they eventually erupt, they become something damaging and harmful to the people around us.

One of the most well-known quotes in every 12-Step program is: "*You've gotta feel it to heal it.*" As someone who absolutely hated feeling anything that made me uncomfortable, this was the best advice I'd ever heard and the single most important tool I started using over the years to process feelings and heal from anything in my life that was hard.

It was in that 12-step program where I learned that all my 'self-control' tactics were an illusion. If I would just allow myself to feel "it," whatever "it" was, I could make peace with it and heal what ailed me.

My mom was the role model I grew up with. Strong. Resilient. Positive and *always* in control. I strived to be like her. Positive and optimistic no matter what life threw my way. We were raised to be strong and resilient, not negative, or ungrateful because somebody out there had it worse than us. The way through life was to remain positive. Glass half full kind of thing. I mean, if she could do it. Why couldn't I?

But I was different. More sensitive. *Overly sensitive.* A tad *too* empathetic. A chronic people pleaser who didn't like to rock the boat or risk anyone not liking me. When I had big feelings, I thought it best to push those feelings right down.

Anger got me into trouble and cost me my childhood best friend. Sadness and tears, especially if they leaked out in the workplace, were "unprofessional". And being anything but positive cramped my Supergirl vibe because I had been praised all my life for how "strong and resilient" I was, and I wanted to live up to people's perception of me.

But the pushing down of the feelings led to things that for periods of time wreaked havoc in my life... Depression. Anxiety. Secrets. Migraines. Illness. Chronic fatigue. Binging. Purging. Starving. Lies. And ultimately not feeling I could be who I truly was and still be loved.

And like every human being that walks this earth, I wanted to be able to be me and still be loved.

Healing doesn't mean the damage or trauma or upset never happened. It means it no longer triggers you and controls your life.

I didn't want the bad things that happened in my life to make me a victim. Bad things happen to everyone, and I saw those things as an opportunity to do some deep inner work on myself. And that work, God it was hard. But as one of my very favorite authors in the world, Glennon Doyle likes to say, "we can do hard things".

The hard thing for me was surrendering to the discomfort, the judgment of others, the judgments I had about myself and owning the truth of who I was and how I actually feel about things.

As I've shared, I went to therapy. I explored yoga and meditation retreats. I dove deep into my Catholic faith and spirituality. I prayed and sat in silence for hours listening for God and then writing what I heard Him say.

I traveled to Peru and Costa Rica where I was introduced to sacred plant medicine, a very big part of those cultures used for healing. These ceremonies invoke guidance from the spiritual world which was totally my jam being I was very woo woo and loved all things connected with the spiritual realm. It was in those ceremonies I was confronted with feelings I didn't realize I had been carrying for years and invited to heal them. I saw visions that *guided me* to making changes I don't think I would have had the courage to make on my own. I still can't explain to anyone who has never participated in a sacred ceremony the power and magic that happens in that space but *wow wow wow*, it completely changed my life and how I viewed everything that has happened to me up to this point.

If you're brave enough to step outside your comfort zone and try different things to open your heart and hold a mirror up to yourself, you'll uncover one simple truth; you've got to feel whatever it is you're running from to heal that thing for good.

For those people who think I have it all together all the time, I want to set the record straight. Nobody has it together all of the time.

To believe that you should, that there is anybody in this world who has "it" ...whatever "it" is together all the time, well that's the very thing that's causing any of us to feel sad, depressed, angry, overwhelmed, suicidal, anxious, (fill in the blank with whatever emotion you feel you shouldn't be feeling today).

I have it together most days. And others I feel completely overwhelmed.

I'm sometimes sad for no reason at all and will allow myself to cry if that's what's needed. Crying I've learned is just a way the body releases what it's holding. It's not good or bad. It's just a release.

I feel sorry for myself at times when life gets challenging, even knowing that somebody else has it worse than me. But I no longer try to shut those feelings down. I let it come, feel it, and let it pass. We all have things in our lives that make us feel sorry for ourselves. We don't need to beat our chests and declare to the world, "I'm FINE" when we aren't but instead accept that it's just a feeling.

And feeling it is not admitting we're weak or pathetic, but *human.*

I get angry. And when I do, I don't make myself out to be a horrible person because of that anger. I sit with it, ask what it's trying to show me about myself or someone else and then I listen to it. I approach it with compassion instead of judgment. Maybe I have a right to be angry. Maybe someone is doing something out of integrity or hurtful and the anger is an invitation for me to stand up for myself, walk away, or learn how to set a boundary.

Every feeling we have is trying to teach us something. I've learned to listen to the teacher and ask, "What are you trying to show me? What's the lesson here?"

I've suffered loss. Experienced betrayals. Navigated heartbreak. Come through the other side of depression. Conquered an eating disorder. All the things and none of the things that others have been through. We all have our things we need to heal from. Mine aren't any harder than yours.

But you *can* heal. You can be happy even if you've been through something traumatic. You can be fully you and still be loved. But you've gotta feel it, to heal it if you want to get there.

Dina Strada

Chapter 21
Get to Know the Full-Bodied Yes

If I'm honest, I said yes to everything for over half my life because I didn't think the word no was an option. Now, I use it all the time. No, I don't want to get a dog. No, I don't want to go to that event. No, I can't take on more work. The greatest form of self-love is getting to know what a full-bodied YES feels like and then saying no to everything else.

I was scrolling through my social media feed one night and I saw his comment under a picture I had posted.

I hadn't heard from him in at least four or five years. A wave of surprise along with a tiny whisper of guilt creeped through my body.

We had dated not long after my divorce. I knew we wanted different things. He shared he had a crush on me for years, but I had only ever viewed him as a friend. Still, he was such a nice guy, I thought, "What the hell," and soldiered on. Hanging out with him couldn't hurt.

We went out on a second date, then a third. I knew I wasn't feeling it. It felt forced. I wasn't feeling anything. I admit I pushed through my hesitation because I felt pressured by well-meaning friends, "It's nice to have someone to go out with," they encouraged me. "You have to give people a chance and he's a great guy," they said.

So, I listened and went against my own intuition. Something I'd spent half my life doing. Pushing down the feelings and going against what I knew in my heart wasn't right for me, like an obedient child I did what I was told. Because maybe, just this one time, I was wrong.

Let me preface this by saying we had a lot of fun together. He checked all of my so-called "boxes"; honest, outgoing, trustworthy, and fun. He was a single parent like me, so he understood my lifestyle and limitations. But something felt off.

It wasn't him. It wasn't me. It just didn't feel right *for* me.

Suffice it to say, when I ended things, he was hurt and a little pissed off. I had let it go on too long because I didn't listen to my own intuition, and I was avoiding a difficult conversation. I wish I could tell you I learned my lesson after him, but I didn't. Every time a "nice guy" came along, and I wasn't feeling it after the first couple dates, I still allowed friends to convince me I was passing judgment too soon and forced myself to go on with it far longer than I knew I should.

I thought maybe it was me. Maybe like working out, I should pass through the discomfort in the hopes I'd eventually feel a connection.

No. No. No. No. We have to learn to start listening to ourselves and our own inner voice—not everyone else's.

I know when the connection is there and when it isn't. I know what it feels like in my body when something feels right. I've been in enough relationships to know the difference between *wanting* to spend time with someone versus feeling I *should want* to spend time with someone.

This goes for everything in our lives, not just relationships. Whether it be a business opportunity, a job, a trip, a big decision about our lives... if it feels like something we *should* do yet we're having the tiniest inkling in our bodies that it isn't right or something feels off...*listen to that. Don't ignore it.*

Get to know what THE SHOULD feels like. We've all felt THE SHOULD. THE SHOULD sucks. THE SHOULD feels like an obligation that makes us do things out of alignment with our souls. THE SHOULD saps our energy and all joy from our interactions with another person. THE SHOULD rears its nasty head and makes us do things we later regret. THE SHOULD needs to be recognized for what it is.

A red light. *Stop.*

A SHOULD sounds like this, "This person really cares about me. They're so nice. I don't want to disappoint them, and I feel like I should give this a chance."

Or "This is such a great opportunity for me. The money is great. The title is what I want. OK, I've heard the person I'd be reporting to threw a stapler at his last assistant and there are a few other red flags, but I'd be crazy not to take it."

Or "This person needs me. They told me nobody else can help them and they're desperate. I'd feel like a horrible person if I don't give in and help them."

THE SHOULD is a *no*. THE SHOULD is your indicator that something isn't a full-bodied yes. THE SHOULD is your sign to hit the pause button, put on the brakes, and ask yourself the question, "Why do I feel I should move forward with this when I know in my heart it's not the right thing for *me?*"

When I work with clients and they ask me what they should do about a particular situation or person, I always turn it back on them. "You know what to do," I say. "When you ask yourself the question, what's the very first thing that comes to mind without trying to explain why you feel that way?" They always have the answer. *We know what is right and what is not for us.*

We know when someone isn't right for us. It's not about the red flags you may see. It's not about whether they possess some list of traits you say you're looking for.

It's an inner knowing in the body.

There should never be a feeling of obligation, guilt, or pressure. If you feel any of those things, it's a no.

This is what a full-bodied yes feels like:
- *Your breathing is even and calm.*
- *There is zero hesitation or second thoughts.*
- *There is no trying to convince yourself.*
- *You're elated, excited, and lit up at the thought of it.*
- *Your body feels centered, balanced, and at peace.*
- *You feel in flow. The energy around it feels harmonious.*

This is what a SHOULD feels like:
- *Your breathing is short and shallow. It feels tight in your chest/heart chakra.*
- *You have to talk yourself into it instead of naturally desiring it.*
- *You feel anxiety, stress, or discomfort in the body.*
- *You experience feelings of resentment or anger.*
- *Your body feels off. You feel unbalanced, off kilter, and confused.*
- *Being with the person feels more like an obligation than joyful.*

It's good to do a gut check with someone you trust when you're trying to determine if something is a should or you're running away out of fear. Some of us have a pattern of running away too soon, but you know yourself.

It's our job to learn to trust ourselves and our own inner compass. Friends and family are great when we need to process and talk things through when we need support, but at the end of the day, we need to learn to trust our own inner knowing.

Hit the pause button when you don't know. Hitting pause is more loving and honest than moving full steam ahead with something you're unsure about. The pause isn't a no. It's a "let's give this some air to breathe."

Sometimes a little more time and checking in with ourselves once we've had time to process what's coming up for us is all we need to make that final right decision for ourselves.

As for my own pattern of saying yes when it's a no, I have finally learned my lesson. Recently I was in another "this feels like a SHOULD instead of a full bodied yes" with someone and found myself wanting to avoid saying no to him to spare his feelings. Instead, I told him how I was feeling from the get-go and although he wasn't happy with how I felt and was a little pissed off he eventually came around and apologized for his reaction to my no.

Just honor how you're feeling and accept that sometimes other people won't be thrilled with your no, but at the end of the day, *you'll* be much happier finally saying adios to all those shitty SHOULDS.

Dina Strada

Chapter 22
You're Exactly Where
You're Meant to Be

If I'm honest, I thought I'd be married by age 26, have my first child by age 30 and write a novel by age 35. I did none of those things at any of those milestones and yet my life has turned out pretty fabulous anyway.

At the writing of this book, I've entered my 5th decade. My life doesn't look at all the way I thought it should.

In my "this is the way it should be" vignette, I'm happily married with 3 kids. I have a cute corgi that my adoring super-hot husband walks every morning around our picture-perfect suburbia neighborhood with our adorable minis traipsing behind him. I've just left my 7-figure job as CEO of some big entertainment conglomerate to work on my next book to follow up my last 4 best-selling novels which all of course all hit the New York Times bestseller list. Also, in this vignette, I'm not yet 40 years old.

Now, obviously my life looks a little different than this. I don't have the cute corgi.

Okaaayyyyyy.... I'm no longer married either. And, well, I haven't made it to a 7-figure salary yet. Or had a CEO title, except as CEO of my own company. And I have some feelings about all that. In my mind, I was supposed to have a different life especially around the idea of being married forever.

When I start to write about my feelings surrounding being a single parent, my initial instinct is to sugar coat it and tell you I'm doing just fine, and it was all "meant to be" so really, I'm totally OK with it. I'll say things like, "It was the best thing for the both of us."

I feel the need to wipe the dirt off the top of the box, shove the crumpled gift inside and slap a pretty red bow around it to make it look prettier than it actually is. Nobody wants to hear me whine about how much I hate being a single mom because there are tons of single parents out there doing their thing just fine. There are also tons of wanna-be parents out there who would give anything just to have kids to whine about.

But I'm not here to wrap a pretty bow around things. The truth is, it's not always pretty. In fact, some days, it's really hard. It also can be very lonely. I don't think we need to put on a show and convince each other that every part of our lives is great when in fact, it's not. I want to give you permission to *also* not love some aspect of your own life but still be able to say, "I didn't see myself here, but I trust it's where I'm supposed to be."

I've made peace with where I'm at because that's where I'm at. Period, end of story. I no longer waste energy focusing on how I think things should be and instead try to enjoy and appreciate where I'm at right now.

I trust where I'm at. I trust that it's Divinely perfect. I surrender to all of it, because I know that it's what my soul chose to experience while here on this earthly place. (Damn you, soul for some of the decisions you made without my input! And yes, this is my *woo woo* belief system coming out). My path is different from yours. Your path is different from anyone else's. There is no such thing as getting to Point A by a certain age and Point B by another age and then traveling a linear path to Point C.

Millennials especially are driving themselves nuts over this stuff. I had lunch recently with a group of them at a conference and they admitted that they've been conditioned to believe that if they haven't made it to a VP level pulling in 6 figures by age 25, they're a failure. When I was 25, I was fetching my boss coffee and filling her car up with gas when she even allowed me to leave my desk lest I miss a very important call for her. The group looked appalled at this confession and that was before I dropped the bomb that I did it all for a mere $32K a year.

I didn't question where I was back then. I trusted my gut. I knew it was leading me somewhere even if that somewhere looked like a foreign country compared to my closest friends and family's lives. When my girlfriends were getting engaged and making lifetime commitments, I was struggling to commit to a 3-year lease on a car.

When my friends were giving birth to their first babies, I was failing miserably at even landing a date.

When they were buying homes, I was scraping together enough money to rent a 1-bedroom apartment I didn't have to share with a perfect stranger I found on Craigs' list.

My point is, I did things a little later than the people surrounding me. I didn't get married until my 30s. Didn't have my first child until age 38. When friends and colleagues were getting promoted into bigger jobs with fancier titles making salaries, I felt I should be making, my career hit a plateau. There were times I thought to myself, "Why am I so behind? Why do things take so much longer to happen for me?"

I had to remind myself over and over again to stop comparing myself to everyone around me, trust my own path and believe things were happening at the perfect time for *me*.

Everything is working out in your favor even when you don't see it. Even when you think you should be doing something or have something right now at this moment in your life. Maybe you think you should be in a relationship by now or have gotten married or pregnant or promoted or be making a certain amount of money.

Trust there's a reason it hasn't materialized yet.

Maybe you're not ready.
Or you don't need it.
Maybe you've got bigger things to accomplish first.
Or you're meant for something more.
Maybe it's just not the right time yet.
Or it's not meant for you.

My favorite mantra whenever I'm anxious about something coming my way is, "*If not this, something better.*" Say it when you're wanting something to manifest in your life.

If not this, something better.

I have a client who wanted to have kids more than anything all through her 30's but hadn't met the right guy to settle down with. By the time she did meet him and get married, she was 44 years old and thought her only option was to adopt, which wasn't exactly what she wanted. "I'm afraid I wouldn't be able to bond with a child I adopt in the same way I would if it were really mine." Every time we had a session together, I'd tell her, "There's a plan for you. Just pray and ask for this or something better."

She and her husband chose to go the adoption route when they were told her chances of conceiving on her own were less than 10%. But their adoption journey was riddled with problems, and they hit roadblock after roadblock. She was now 45 years old and had been taking fertility drugs as a backup plan. Every time I talked to her, she was discouraged and felt defeated. At one point she told me, "I think it's too late for me. Maybe I'm not meant to have a family."

But something better was in store for her.

Right before her 46th birthday, she found out she was pregnant with twins! And 9 months after she had twins, they adopted a baby girl.

The kids are now all teenagers. When I asked her if I could share her story, she was more than happy to give someone else hope, "Every one of my kids was meant to be ours. I can't imagine our family without each one of them and can't believe I ever thought I wouldn't love my adopted daughter as much as the twins. I'm *so in love* with all of them and proof that things happen when they're supposed to in ways you never dream are possible."

I think of her every time I'm waiting for something to happen in my own life. And then remind myself, "If not this, something better will come."

Chapter 23
Validation is an Inside Job

If I'm honest, I spent most of my life looking for validation outside myself that I was good enough. It was the biggest waste of time ever.

For most of my life, I felt good or bad about myself based on what another person said to me. It started in kindergarten.

My teacher Mrs. Nutt made me put my head down on my desk one day after I accidentally tripped another boy, telling me I was careless and should now spend the next hour thinking about what I did. I still remember that day instead of the 100 other days I was praised by her for my conscientiousness and hard work. I felt bad and "careless" as she called me, and the whole class knew it.

I was a fantastic student in school, but I only felt smart when I got an A or a teacher praised me. A written letter grade on paper determined how smart I actually felt rather than me knowing it in my core. I felt special only when I was sought out to receive some kind of special award. I felt pretty only when someone commented that I looked good, and I felt good about who I was as a person only when another person was gushing over how fabulous I was.

But never did I see how deeply I sought validation outside myself than when I became a mother. As the years went on, I trusted and knew I was smart, talented, a good friend, a loyal daughter, and a hard-working and dedicated employee. But when I became a mother, I was searching everywhere outside myself for validation that I was doing it right.

I needed to hear it from my own mother because she was the high bar I set for myself. And I especially looked for it from my kids' father.

I don't know why I needed to hear it so much from him but after we divorced, I found I was constantly seeking some kind of acknowledgement or validation that I was good at something since his leaving had left me feeling not good enough.

It wasn't just around my parenting skills I sought his approval. I needed to hear him say he thought I was a good wife, an amazing person and that he regretted the decision he made to split up. I wanted him to tell me he remembered all the good times we had together and how happy I once made him. Just some gesture that he respected me and saw my worth.

Over the years I began to realize my need for validation from him was about my own insecurities. Why did I need *him* to tell me I was good enough? What did it matter what he or anyone else thought of me?

As I started the long process of healing and wanting to become better for myself, I became aware of how often I looked outside myself for validation that I was a good person and doing a good job in every area of my life. Work. Friendships. Family. Parenting. *Where was my own internal compass to make these determinations? Why did I feel somebody else needed to approve of me to feel good about myself?*

So, I worked hard on this for years until it became a practice. The work was in trusting *myself*, and what I knew to be right for me, not what other people thought I should be doing. It was getting quiet in moments of confusion and uncertainty and learning to listen to my *own voice and intuition, not somebody else's*. We know what's best for ourselves and what works for our lives.

Walk that path.

Trust in it and trust yourself. Trust your own inner compass. Our deepest work is standing firm in that trust and not wavering when somebody else doesn't agree with, support or has an opinion about what we're doing or who we are. We know who we are.

True happiness and inner peace come when we learn to love and accept ourselves for exactly who we are. Every single part of us. Every flaw, every mistake, every imperfection. When we love that person, we don't need anyone's approval.

Every time we get upset because of what someone else says about us, we're saying, "what you think of me is more important than what I think of myself". It gives another person way too much power over you.

I remember the moment I stopped giving away my power. I had gotten to a place where I felt like I was doing a phenomenal job raising my kids, setting boundaries on my time, showing up for my life and being as authentic and kind as I could in my relationships. Someone hurled an insult at me about my character after I set a boundary with them. I remember not flinching one tiny bit. The thing that person said about me wasn't true at all. I know who I am and although they're entitled to feel however they want, it doesn't make what they said true.

Before I would obsess about it. I would question myself and start to believe whatever that other person said about me. If they said it, it must be true. I must be that person.

Not this time. And not any time after that day. Today I can stand solid in who I am and although I seek out other people's opinions who I trust when I need support or advice, I don't need their approval if I choose to take a different path.

The best advice I've ever received when someone shares their unsolicited opinion around what I'm doing and I don't agree with them is, "Thanks so much for the feedback." That's it. There's nowhere to go with that response, no need to defend myself or argue with them. Just thank them for sharing and move the heck on with your life.

You do you. Let that be your mantra. You don't need anyone's approval on how you choose to live your life. Put those fabulous words, **"Thanks for the feedback"** on the palm of your hand. Then hold that baby up and wave *bye Felicia* the next time anyone gives you their unsolicited opinion on you or your life.

Just do you.

Chapter 24
Acceptance is the Answer to All My Problems

If I'm honest, not accepting a person or situation in my life is what has caused me the greatest amount of pain and suffering. Luckily, I found the secret weapon to curing that ailment in a simple prayer I recite to this day.

"When I am disturbed, it is because I find some person, place, or situation – some fact of my life – unacceptable to me, and I can find no serenity until I accept that person, place, thing, or situation as being exactly the way it is supposed to be at this moment. Nothing, absolutely nothing, happens in God's world by mistake. Until I could accept (insert whatever you're struggling with), I could not abstain; unless I accept life completely on life's terms, I cannot be happy. I need to concentrate not so much on what needs to be changed in the world as on what needs to be changed in me and my own attitudes." - *Acceptance Prayer, Big Book of Alcoholics Anonymous*

Yep, just read that bad boy a few times. It's epic. And it has the ability to literally transform your life.

If you look at any person or situation in your life right now that's causing you grief, anxiety or upset, it's most likely because you want them or it to be different. You simply can't accept them or the situation for what it is.

Can you relate?

I found I struggled with this most in my twenties and early thirties and most often in relationships. Most of us have a need to mold people according to our own desires and needs and this is always going to backfire on us and leave us feeling like hell.

In my late twenties, all my friends had met "the one". It was a season of excitement, gushing over friend's diamond rings and romantic engagement stories, picking out bridesmaids' dresses together, attending bridal showers and elbowing those other single ladies outta my way during the bouquet toss.

I was feeling the heat. The heat to meet *the one*. So, when I started dating somebody who checked all my boxes on paper, I was hopeful. He was a great guy. Smart, artistic, witty, funny with a huge heart and a deep love for me. As wonderful as he was though, we had absolutely nothing in common. He was a super laid-back artist into motorcycles, retro cars with a vintage 1960s style who preferred to relax and spend time alone.

I was the opposite. A Type A personality who spent most of my time making to-do lists, running myself up my own asshole, whose style was Crate and Barrel and Pottery Barn. I didn't know *how* to relax. I mean, my hobbies involved running, working out, entering 5K races around southern California and accepting every social invitation that came my way, then dragging him along for the ride.

I loved him and wanted to get married so dammit I was determined to fit that square peg into the round hole. He admitted he was a bit of a commitment-phobe right from the get-go, and marriage wasn't something he was sure he wanted. But I had plans and my plans involved changing his mind.

And changing him.

I didn't know the first thing about accepting someone or something for who they are.   I didn't accept that he didn't want to get married. I couldn't accept that he was on the fence about having kids one day. I refused to accept that he was at times messy and didn't see the point in making the bed in the morning or paying bills on time. I didn't accept his taste, or style or that he preferred to watch a movie at home rather than attend a party or social event with me. I was in that horrible place of non-acceptance with what was, so it may come as no surprise that it was during this time in my life, I relapsed into my eating disorder.

I didn't like not having control over this situation, so I took back some control by attempting to control my food intake and my body.

It was a time of absolute misery. On the outside of course I pretended everything was great. But inside I was depressed, scared, frantic and miserable. Rock bottom led me right back into therapy and OA, the 12 Step program where I learned about acceptance, for myself, other people, and the world around me. I worked with a sponsor, attended at least 3 meetings a week, and worked those 12 steps like my life depended on it. Which in many ways, it did.

Along with that work, I was introduced to yoga and meditation through a close friend. Sitting still was *not my jam*. I hated it. I wanted to run screaming from the room after 15 minutes of savasana. But the practice of laying on a mat where I had to sit with my own thoughts instead of escaping them through food, controlling things around me or pretending that everything was OK is what led me to start looking at *my* part in my own unhappiness.

I realized I was the problem, not him. I hadn't been willing to accept him and the relationship for what it was. I was holding onto him out of fear I would never find someone else or get married instead of trusting that everything would work out if I surrendered to the unknown and just trusted in things. We made great friends but were too different to make it as a couple. And me trying to change him was so unfair to him and didn't make him feel good. We all just want to be loved and accepted for who we are, not what someone else wants us to be.

I share this very story with a lot of young girls I work with in their twenties who are frantic that they're still single and watching everyone around them getting married. I see that look of desperation and panic in their eyes as they tell me they can't bear to attend another wedding without feeling like they're going to break down in hysterics.

For the love of God girls, let me be a lesson to you. Don't panic and settle for a square peg. Don't think you're running out of time. And don't waste time staying in a relationship trying to change that person into who you need and want them to be to make your relationship work. It won't work. Ever.

I still have people in my life who aren't my cup of tea or I don't vibe with. And I still deal with situations I wish were different. I don't like doing everything on my own all the time, but I've accepted it. I hate that my father's health has declined rapidly in the past year, but I've accepted it. I'm vastly different from certain friends of mine in lifestyle, political beliefs and how we see the world, but I accept them for who they are. They show me a different way to look at things. The difference between now and who I was 20 years ago is I no longer expend any energy wishing, wanting, praying, and bitching that they are different to suit who I am.

"I need to concentrate not so much on what needs to be changed in the world as on what needs to be changed in me and my own attitudes." This is the line from the Big Book of Alcoholics Anonymous I always go back to when I'm struggling. Because my own thoughts and attitude about things are really the only thing I have any control over at all.

Chapter 25
Let Your Freak Flag Fly

If I'm honest...I think fitting in when you get to be an adult is boring. I deeply admire people who stand out. The ones who aren't afraid to be who they are, boldly take chances and walk the path others think are crazy. Those are my people.

Word had made its way through the building that *Brad* (yes, that Brad) was in the house. This was just a few years after his butt made its glorious debut in the movie *Legends of the Fall*, and he was the hottest actor in Hollywood.

Whispers of what conference room he was headed to and the location of his next stop on the studio tour quickly made its way through the assistant's desks and before you knew it, everyone suddenly had to relieve their bladders and use the ladies room located around the corner from where Brad was currently being shown storyboards of our upcoming animated film *Sinbad*.

I, of course, wanted to get a good look at Brad's butt myself but didn't want to be *that* girl. If you work for a movie studio, you're not supposed to be a fan girl. Besides, I was too afraid of what my bosses might think if I tried to pull a sly one and saunter through the hallway where they were gathered as I pretended that I needed to use the bathroom right around the corner.

Said bosses wouldn't have noticed either way because they were too busy trying to make a good impression on Brad while distracting him from the 3-ring circus now happening in the hallway as every rando employee casually made their way past him on their way to faux meetings that everyone knew weren't actually happening.

Since I didn't want to walk past Brad for no good reason, I started chugging water at my desk until my bladder was so full, I legitimately *had* to use the ladies' room which meant moseying on down to the 2nd floor to use the one right around the corner from where all the action was happening. And I got my lookie loo of the famous and unforgettable, Brad Pitt.

Was it worth it? Hell ya! Did I do it again over the course of the 20+ years I worked in Hollywood and brushed shoulders with Hollywood's elite?

Hell ya!

Brad Pitt became one of the hundreds of actors and celebrities I pretended over the years to not fangirl over while living in LA and working for a movie studio. Because fangirling at work is not allowed. We were expected to be *professional.*

Professional is a word I hate. Be professional. Look professional. Act professional. I get that's a thing for people but it's not my thing.

Yet, I've managed to be professional enough throughout my career to work my way up the corporate ladder at some big companies; King World Productions, ABC-TV, DreamWorks Animation and NBCUniversal. I'm not implying that being professional is a thing I don't want to do, nor do I believe I would be where I am today without exercising some degree of professionalism. My point is that people's opinions of what's professional in the workplace and what's not can be all over the map.

Which brings me to one of the biggest things I've struggled with and maybe you do too, and that's *doing me and not worrying what people think about that.*

I wanna be me and do what lights me up. I don't want to push down parts of myself I think are cool because other people may not think it's cool.

My struggle over the years has been feeling it's Ok to be one hundred percent myself inside the corporate environment. I'm a writer which is a vulnerable profession and often feels like running naked through the streets every time I write and publish something. I'm also an intuitive and a life coach which is my passion and what I do outside my day job. But for much of my career, I felt I couldn't allow those parts of myself to be seen because I wanted to be taken seriously.

I hid that I was intuitive because people who knew this little factoid about me would often joke that I was a witch and call me psychic and that word turns me off. The word psychic conjures up images of those crazy 1-800-DIAL-A-PSYCHIC hotlines for $2 a minute and I'm definitely not one of those! Besides, many people have very strong opinions about psychics, not good ones, so I was hesitant for people at work to know I dabbled in any of that stuff.

One time, a producer I worked with at DreamWorks blurted out to an entire room of executives including one who was pregnant, "Dina knows the sex of every baby born here so if you want to know what you're having ask her because she's a WIIIITCHHHHH!"

Not how I wanted to be seen by my colleagues, but now everyone had the witch image of me impaled in their brains. And now I had the added pressure of having to accurately predict the sex of DreamWorks babies since it had been broadcast all over the studio. (Fun fact: I have a 98% accuracy rate but of course got it wrong for my own kids).

Eventually, I started to become more open with select people about my witchy ways, my love of tarot cards, astrology, full moon ceremonies and manifestation rituals. I did all the things and was giving friends and co-workers readings on the down low. I loved doing it because it helped people and besides, I was good at it. During lunch, people would sneak into my office under the guise that we had a meeting. They'd ask me questions about their careers, their relationships, or their marriages. Super juicy shit.

One time I picked up that there was an affair going on between someone I was reading and another person in the office which blew their minds (and mine) and before I knew it, word got out I was really and truly a full-blown PSYCHIC (that word I hate) and then I couldn't keep up with all the requests for readings! I started getting booked for Hollywood parties, the Emmys gifting suite and even a well-known actors' private birthday party and although I was flattered, I still wanted to keep the whole thing on the down low.

What would the executives who resided on the 2nd floor think?

My point is, no matter how much we may want to keep some part of ourselves hidden, eventually the real you is gonna come out. And you know what? People are probably gonna LOVE IT. Maybe fitting in was all the rage when you were in middle school, but standing out is where it's at when you grow up!

Think about the greatest entrepreneurs out there. They're the ones who think outside the box and stand out. Are you really paying attention to anyone who just blends in with the crowd? Probably not. Don't make yourself small or think you need to pick one thing in the world to be and stick to that one thing your whole life. You can be the CEO of a Fortune 500 company and also be into astrology. You can be a graphic designer and also do photography as your side hustle. You can be a nurse and sell vintage farmhouse signs on Etsy. Or work as a financial analyst and start your own interior design business on the side.

Do you, be you and kick the whole idea to the curb that nobody will take you seriously if you let your freak flag fly or allow your creative side out into the world. Most people will admire you for it and be inspired by your courage. At the end of the day, we're all just looking to each other for permission to be who we are. So, give someone else permission to be who they are by having the guts to be yourself.

Dina Strada

Chapter 26
Just Do the Damn Thing

If I'm honest, I can't believe the cajónes I had to write what I'm about to share below.

April 30, 1995

Jeffrey Katzenberg
DreamWorks SKG
100 Universal Plaza
Universal City, CA 91608

Dear Mr. Katzenberg,

I know that the response to your new studio has been overwhelming and you have been inundated with resumes and phone calls. Add another to the pile but keep this one on top because you won't find anyone else with my drive, energy, passion, and perseverance. Since hearing of the creation of DreamWorks, I have been hell-bent on getting the opportunity to work for "la creme de la cream" of the entertainment industry. I will do ANYTHING, and I mean ANYTHING to get my foot in the door. If that means making coffee for you, David Geffen and Steven Spielberg before morning meetings or polishing the conference room table, I'll do it!!

I'm currently working in the Affiliate Relations Department at Capital Cities/ABC and understand that DreamWorks has made a deal with Bob Iger to produce original live action programming for the network. With my years of experience in television on both the syndication and network level as well as my experience working in the music industry, I feel I have much to offer DreamWorks in terms of diversity and experience. I am particularly interested in working in the film division of DreamWorks and would welcome any opportunity to become a part of your team.

I know that chances are, you are still in the early stages of development and aren't yet looking to hire staff right now. However, I am writing in the hopes that you will pull my resume when the time comes to hire bright, hard-working new talent to launch DreamWorks' first projects. Though I may not be one of the first people you hire in the coming months to start up your first projects, I will always keep in mind what you said to Dawn Steel when she was working for you at Paramount Pictures, "If they throw you out the front door, you go in the back door, and if they throw you out the back door you go in the window, and if they throw you out the window you go in the basement. And you don't ever take it personally." I won't give up until I make it through DreamWorks' door!

Thank you in advance for your consideration. I hope to hear from you soon.

Sincerely,

Dina Strada

This was the letter I wrote to Jeffrey Katzenberg back in 1995, who at the time had stepped down from his Chairman post at Walt Disney Studios to start up his own film studio with director Steven Spielberg and business magnate, producer, and studio executive David Geffen. The studio was DreamWorks SKG. At the time, I didn't think a recent college grad writing a personal letter to a big studio mogul was a big thing, but apparently it was.

My friends thought it was *ballsy*.

And yea, I guess it was. But back then I didn't think twice about not going after the things I wanted. I believed if I didn't at least try, how would I get it? If I didn't put myself out there, how could anything good find me?

So, at 24 years old, I wrote this ballsy letter and somebody in Mr. Katzenberg's office actually read it and thought it was fabulous. The Head of HR at DreamWorks called me and said, "Your letter was so creative. We loved it! If you're going to be in the LA area, we'd love to meet you for an informational interview. We're just starting the hiring process."

Well, wouldn't you know, my roommate, Nicole who worked in the record industry at the time happen to be taking a business trip to LA two weeks later and had invited me along to see if I even liked LA since I had been blabbering on and on about leaving NYC and moving there one day. The timing was incredible and definitely a sign from God.

I flew out to LA with Nicole and went into DreamWorks for an interview. There was an opening to be Jeffrey Katzenberg's 2nd Assistant that the Head of HR thought I would be great for, although maybe a little over-qualified. I felt I wanted to work in Publicity or Marketing and said I was willing to hold out for something else. She told me they were in the process of hiring all the executives in the next 6 months and those execs would need assistants so to please keep in touch and they'd find me something.

It was the *longest* 9 months of my life. Worse than being pregnant! All I thought about was this impossible dream I had of working for DreamWorks. It was the hottest new studio in town, in what I thought was the most glamorous, coolest city ever (I didn't yet know about the blazing fires, mudslides, smog or horrendous traffic I'd later come to hate). I had grown weary of living in New York and being dirt poor, eating only carbs 3 meals a day because fresh produce and meat cost way too much, wading through drifts of snow during the winter to make it to the cross-town bus to get to work and breathing in some guy's body odor as my 4'11" body was crushed beneath total strangers on the subway in the oppressive heat of summer.

They didn't call me. I called them. I was persistent as hell. I followed up every 2-3 months to check in and see where they were at in the hiring process and remind them that I was still very much interested in working there and ready to come onboard when the right role opened up. I had zero fear and zero ego. I never once thought "what will they think of me for being so persistent?" I compare the person I was then, to the person I am now and think, "*Who was that girl who wasn't afraid to go after something and not give a damn what anyone else thought?*"

And because of that, I landed the job of my dreams that was the beginning of my entire career.

They asked if I could be out in LA in 3 weeks. It was absolute insanity. I sublet my apartment to my friend Linda and sold everything I owned. I didn't have time to be scared that I was leaving my friends and family and knew absolutely no one in LA or come up with a list of excuses of why I shouldn't move 3,000 miles across the country to a city I knew nothing about. The thought never crossed my mind that I could fail or that I wasn't good enough or that I didn't deserve to have what I wanted.

I just did the damn thing.

And because I did, I had a life that exceeded my wildest imagination. I didn't just *meet* Jeffrey Katzenberg, I got to work closely with him for over 20 years on dozens of animated films. From sitting in on story meetings and editorial sessions where we developed and cut the film, to accompanying him on his private jet to do recording sessions with

Robert DeNiro, Will Smith, Renée Zellweger and Martin Scorsese, to sitting in meetings with Steven Spielberg to hear his notes on a cut of our latest film, to pitching storyboards to some of my all-time favorite R&B recording artists of all time in a NYC hotel suite (can you say Janet Jackson if you're nasty baby?)

I met every person I ever dreamed of meeting in that job. I shared a ride from NYC to LA on a private jet with Chris Rock who *needed a ride home.* I was given the task of escorting the cast of Modern Family to a step and repeat photo op at an Emmy Party. I rubbed shoulders with JLo and Marc Anthony on the red carpet at a screening of our animated film *Home.* (yes, she is just as gorgeous in person). One memorable evening I was given the task of guarding Leonardo DiCaprio's VIP lounge area where he sat with Steven Spielberg all night and was so close to them I could count the hairs on his head. Great hair btw Leo! I tried not to fangirl when I got into a whole conversation with Edie Falco while wrist banding her at a party on our favorite *Sopranos* moments.

But the bucket list item of all was, wait for it... doing a recording session with Oprah who was a voice in our animated film *Bee movie.*

Once I walked the halls of Harpo studios, sat on the couch in her greenroom drinking a Perrier and sat in the audience to watch a taping of her show when the cast of Seinfeld was on, I decided then and there I could die and go to Heaven although I was pretty sure Heaven couldn't hold a candle to being 10 feet from Oprah.

Anyway, my point is, I would never have done all these things and more had I not done the thing I was most scared to do. I could never have lived the life I did, one which by the way I *couldn't even imagine for myself,* if I had let my fear of being rejected or not getting what I want stop me.

If I'm honest, when I was writing this chapter, I had originally planned to share that writing this book was the thing I couldn't do. I've had this book in me for years. I had never in my life wanted to do something so much, but truly felt I wasn't good enough to do it.

I thought I wasn't talented enough, witty enough, or original enough or marketable enough. I thought I had nothing to say that hadn't been said before by some other great writer. I thought it was an unrealistic dream to write a book because I still work a day job I love while balancing my coaching business and clients *and* raising 2 kids. I thought I was too busy. I believed I didn't have a big enough social media following and I didn't want to have to do all the things required to build a following because that goes against who I am, which is a "people will find me" kinda gal.

My point is, I was stuck in the now instead of remembering who I truly am. If that 24-year-old girl could be brazen enough to write to the head of one of the biggest studios in Hollywood and ask for a job, and then *get the job* then why couldn't I after accomplishing every unimaginable dream I've had for myself for the past 20 plus years not just do THIS. ONE. THING.

You can do anything. You can be anything. I don't say this because I'm trying to shove some positive woo woo "you can do it" shit down your throat. I say it because you *actually can.*

If you don't do the thing you've dreamt of doing your entire life, you'll regret it. I promise, you *will* regret it. The only difference between you and someone else you're watching doing the very thing you want to do is simply that person took action. They made the choice to just do the damn thing. Trust me when I tell you that same person was also scared as hell, and probably didn't believe they could make the leap to whatever it is they're doing now.

But they did it anyway.

Acknowledgements

Let me start by acknowledging how hard this book was to actually write. I stopped and started more times than I can count, repeatedly told my closest friends and writing coach and mentor, Monika Carless, I didn't even want to write a damn book (even though I did) and kicked and screamed along the way. Quite frankly, it's a miracle it ever happened and that you're holding this bad boy in your hands.

So, thank you first and foremost to my friend Monika Carless for pushing me to do this. Monika and I met while writing articles for *elephant journal* back in 2015, when we were both competing each month for the top writer spot. I voraciously read all of her stuff and wanted to know who this talented, prolific writer was and then plotted how I could beat her, only to find out she equally loved my own work and wanted to know more about me. A friendship and supportive mutual mentorship was born. As coaches and intuitives, we've worked together, done readings and coaching sessions for each other and always been each other's biggest cheerleader. Monika, I am deeply grateful to you for helping me navigate through some of the more challenging moments in my life and offering your wise words and advice when I needed it most. Thank you for patiently and gently kicking my Jersey ass to get this thing birthed. Brad Pitt has nothing on you!

To my bestie, Elizabeth Walsh, who spent many evenings in deep process with me, notebook in hand, jotting down all my ideas for the content, structure and purpose of this book and sharing her own. Thank you for believing in me, encouraging me, cheering me on, reading what I sent you, sharing your suggestions and helping me make it better. But more importantly, thank you for being the person who helped me heal so much of what I've shared in this book so I can now pass it onto others. I love you.

To Daniel Zamilpa, my QUEEN and the creative mind behind all things marketing/social media. Thank you for helping me get this thing into the world and generously giving your time, energy, and advice to make it the best it could be. I adore you more than you'll ever know. Step that P-SSY UP!

My sister, Nicole Forcellati, doesn't love reading but read everything I sent her anyway! I appreciate it more than you know.

My brother Remo, for not making fun of the title, pretending he might actually read the book one day (I have my doubts), and designing such a kick ass cover.

Rodolphe Guenoden, my dear friend from DreamWorks Animation and one of the most talented artists I know for designing the adorable caricature of me for the book cover and always being one of the biggest advocates and supporters of my writing over the years. I didn't think men read my work but loved that you took the time to read mine and share your thoughts on it. Mwah!

Chip Sullivan, thank you for saving the letter I wrote to Jeffrey in a file in your office for all those years. I used to be embarrassed when you relentlessly teased me about it but now, I realize it's one of the bravest things I've ever done (next to allowing the PAs to hang a string of panties outside your office door).

To all my friends and family who encouraged me for years and said, "I can't wait till you write your book!" Well, here it is, so I hope you love it. Neil VanHarte, Linda Giambrone, Nicole Giambrone, Nicole Frances, Carol Adler, Deanne Koehn, Kerry Textor, Ariella Bimbi, Patrick Llewellyn, Matt Flugger, Leslie Smalley-Davis, Patty Colangelo, Diane Wooley, Harriet Dispenziere, Laurie Gowen, Mariana Lopez. You each know what you've done to get me here and how grateful I am for you. Other friends, if I forgot you here, please forgive me. I am grateful for every one of you.

Mom and dad, thank you for your unwavering love, support, generosity, encouragement and always being there for me and the kids. I couldn't do life without you. You taught me I could do anything, so Oprah better call me after this book is released, and yes mom, I promise you can come with me.

Last but not least, my loves Logan and Kaia, you are my everything and put up with lots of late nights, uncooked dinners and obsessive talking about this book and my dreams for it. Thank you for being as excited for me to birth it into the world as I am. I hope when you actually do read it one day, it will inspire you to go after every dream you have in your own lives.

And to Hoda and Jenna...here I come! Can't wait to meet you.

Dina Strada

About the Author

DINA STRADA is an event producer and Intuitive Coach specializing in relationships, healing, and empowering women. A born and raised Jersey girl, she lived and worked in Hollywood for over 20 years at DreamWorks Animation and NBCUniversal. A former featured author and top writer for *Elephant Journal*, she's penned hundreds of articles and has appeared in *HuffPost*, *Tiny Buddha*, *Thought Catalog*, *Elite Daily*, *The Good Men Project*, *Your Tango*, *Medium*, *Chopra*, *Simply Women*, *Rebelle Society*, and *Thrive Global*. She was a featured author in the book, *Simply Woman: Stories from 30 magnificent women who have risen against the odds*.

Dina resides on the Jersey Shore with her two kids, Logan and Kaia.

You can find more about her at dinastrada.com
Instagram: @Dinamstrada
Facebook: Dina Strada, A Work of Heart